Mary,
the Faithful Disciple

Bertrand Buby, S.M.

D0169585

Paulist Press † New York † Mahwah

Library of Congress
Catalog Card Number: 85-60290

ISBN: 0-8091-2703-2

Published by Paulist Press
997 Macarthur Boulevard
Mahwah, New Jersey 07430

Printed and bound in the
United States of America

Mary,

the Faithful Disciple

Contents

CONTENTS

*"What you have as heritage
take now as task;
for thus you will make it
your own."*

Faust / Goethe

Panorama of:
The Marian Texts and
Selected Texts on Discipleship

I. **MARY IN THE NEW TESTAMENT:**

1. Paul:
   Philippians 2:6–7
   Romans 1:3–4
   Galatians 1:19; 4:4; 4:28–29

2. Mark:
   3:31–35; 6:1–6a; (15:40, 47 & 16:1)?

3. Matthew:
   1:1–17; 1:18–25; 2:11, 13–14, 20–21; 12:46–
   50; 13:53–58

4. Luke:
   1 & 2: Infancy Narratives esp.
   1:26–38; 1:39–56; 2:1–20; 2:21–40; 2:41–
   52; 3:23; 4:22; 8:19–21; 11:27–28

   Acts: 1:14

5. John:
   1:13; 2:1–12; 6:42; 7:1–10; 7:41–43; 8:41;
   19:25–28a

II. DISCIPLESHIP TEXTS:

1. Mark:
   2:13–17; 8:31–35; 9:30–32; 10:32–45

2. Matthew:
   4:18–22; 5:13–16; 8:19–22; 9:9–13; 10:34–42; 16:24–28; 19:23–30

3. Luke:
   5:1–11; 6:12–16; 9:23–24; 9:43–49; 9:57–62; 10:1–9; 14:25–33; 22:28–30

4. John:
   1:35–41; 12:24–26; 13:13–17; 14:1–7; 15:9–17; 17:9–19

Why Another Book on Mary?

Marian devotion was a strong and very personal part of the faith life of Catholics of the previous generation. Both they and the present generation can profit from a new devotion in Marian sentiment, especially if it springs from two important sources: the Sacred Scriptures and the concept of Church and Mary's role within it as Vatican Council II understands her role. This book will focus on Mary as she is seen from the biblical data given in the New Testament and from her role as a forerunner in discipleship. The texts, though limited in number, are rich in potential for creative insights on the person of Mary as a disciple, and as a woman of faith.

Marian devotion that is based solidly on scriptural evidence will make sense to all Christians and will especially supply a source for a meaningful spirituality for Catholics, since Mary is an integral part of their tradition. Many from the last generation of Catholics feel confused, some perhaps betrayed, by what seems to them a diminishing of devotion to Mary. Priests of that generation want to know what they are to preach about Mary. Teachers are concerned how to instruct children about her.

Many lay people find themselves in a transition stage without bearings. They have come to recognize earlier novenas and May crownings as expressive of a piety of childhood and have grown certain that such devotions are inadequate to present adult needs, but they do not know what to substitute.

On the other hand, young Catholics, in a new time with new needs, want to know why Mary must be treated as so important at all. Many young women, for example, find Mary portrayed as a submissive, passive personality, and wonder how she can speak to the active self-determining woman of today.

A scriptural approach to Mary will show her as a very human woman who emerged in a male-dominated culture as a strong individual who followed her Son Jesus in a manner that compared with and even surpassed the disciples of Jesus. She will have all of the characteristics of a disciple and will be faithful to that call of the Lord as we follow her in the New Testament. Some major characteristics of a Marian biblical devotion will be seen from the texts in which she is present or named. Mary's own discipleship can serve as a paradigm for ours without its being either a saccharine one or an out-of-reach image of her as a person.

I am convinced that Mary still has an important role in the Church today, but the emphasis has to be different. Mary is seen much more as a model believer within the Church, as a leading member of a praying community, rather than outside the Church facing the community or on a pedestal within the Church. In a word, Mary, as a faithful believer and disciple, first receives redemption from Jesus Christ before she can bring and offer that same salvation of her Son to others.

This scriptural book on Mary is meant to make you

4

aware of a new approach to her that will help you share who she is and what she means in your life with others, especially with younger people. This book should also help you describe her to those who are not members of the Catholic Church since you will be seeing her within a scriptural context.

But, you may add, why another book on Mary? Am I caught up in the saying of St. Anselm, "There's never enough said or written about Mary"? Not really. I am, like you, trying to live our faith in the person of Jesus in a way adapted to the needs of our times. Ever since Vatican II, we, as the people of God, are called to a dynamic way of living which is faith-inspired and solidly based on the fundamental sources of Catholicism: the Sacred Scriptures and a sound, vibrant and living Church tradition. Our Marian spirituality is an essential part of an integrated revitalization of the Church; hence, this book on Mary.

We may ask: What has happened to the Marian devotions with which we were once so familiar? After the proclamation of the Assumption of Mary (1950), Marian devotion soared to its heights in the mid-1950's—an era of pilgrimages to Lourdes and Fatima, an intense interest in apparitions elsewhere, novenas inspired by the Miraculous Medal, books, articles, and numerous pamphlets, as well as the development of Marian art—and all this brought an exaggerated enthusiasm about Mary.

Suddenly, in the 1960's all of the above developments started to diminish, and some even disappeared. The atmosphere was no longer so enthusiastically Marian, such as we had been accustomed to, and so many experienced a let-down when they noticed more reticence about Mary.

Certain leaders and theologians in the Church, however, soon began to lay the foundation for a new in-depth spirituality concerning Mary, the Mother of God. Chapter

VIII of the document on the Constitution of the Church, enacted by Vatican Council II and basically encouraged by Pope John XXIII and Pope Paul VI, was entirely given over to a consideration of Mary, her importance, her holiness, and her special place in the Church. The insights of the Council were based on a biblical theology of Mary, Mother of God, Mother of the Church and our Mother.

Slowly an upswing in Marian interest began. The United States Conference of Catholic Bishops, on November 21, 1973, issued its pastoral letter on the Blessed Virgin Mary entitled "Behold Your Mother," presenting Mary to us as a woman of faith. This continued biblical approach to the consideration of Mary intends to acquaint us with Mary through the Sacred Scriptures. After all, it is for us that the Scriptures were written, and Mary comes to us primarily through the revealed word of God in the New Testament.

Ten years after Vatican II, Pope Paul VI issued another document in the form of an Apostolic Exhortation entitled "Devotion to the Blessed Virgin Mary." Once more the Scriptures, especially as they are given to us in the liturgy, are the foundation for the balance and development of an authentic devotion to Mary. Shortly after these various official communications, Scripture scholars began to bring out studies of Mary which would lead us into the twenty-first century. Some of the more important works of these writers will be found in an appendix to this book.

WHY IS A RENEWED MARIAN DEVOTION BASED ON THE SCRIPTURES NEEDED FOR THE PEOPLE OF GOD TODAY?

Our children are the future of the Church in this world. Just as they are aware of the new trends in our culture and take them for granted, so our Marian devotion, too, must adapt to their new needs. The present generation desires something that is more responsive to our search for God. We want what is purely sentimental removed from our relationship to Mary and what is repetitive in it replaced with something more dynamic and inviting. All of us are becoming more and more aware that Vatican II has added a depth of theology, pastoral concern, and integration to Mary's role within our lives as the people of God.

Today we are hungering and thirsting for the word of God as it comes to us in the Scriptures. Over these recent years we have taken upon ourselves, perhaps in a way that we never have in the past, the reading of the Scriptures, reflecting upon the message that they have for us and applying the lessons they give to our own personal lives. In our hunger and thirst for God we are responding to the invitation of Jesus who called out to the people of all time:

> If anyone thirsts, let him come to me; let him drink who believes in me. Scripture has it: From within him rivers of living water shall flow (Jn 7:37–38).

We identify ourselves as Church through biblical images and models. We are the "people of God," "pilgrims," "disciples of the Lord Jesus," "believers," and the "body of Christ." As members of the Church and as individuals, we want to focus on the Christ of the Scriptures no matter what the devotion, and who can better help us to do this than Mary who comes to us through the Scriptures as the Mother of Jesus, the woman of faith, the disciple of the Lord?

THE GOSPELS AND MARY

The Gospels present Mary to us under different images and with a focus on her quality as a disciple-believer in Jesus. These differences as they come to us through the four evangelists help us to grow in our knowledge of Mary, to deepen our understanding of her and to learn from her own discipleship something, at least, of what our discipleship to the Lord should be. Today such a pluralistic imaging of Mary is more important, it would seem to me, than a mere stereotyped model of the Mother of Jesus more removed from the primary source of the Scriptures.

IS MARY A DISCIPLE OF THE LORD?

In the important Marian document written by Pope Paul VI, "Devotion to the Blessed Virgin" (February 1964), Mary is spoken of as a disciple of Jesus. The Holy Father's statement is a reflection taken from St. Luke's Gospel; it is an encouragement for the faithful believer to imitate Mary in the call to discipleship:

> Rather she is held up as an example to the faithful for the way in which in her own particular life she fully and responsibly accepted the will of God, because she heard the word of God and did it, and because charity and spirit of service were the driving force of her actions. She is worthy of imitation because she was the first and most perfect of Christ's disciples ("Devotion to the Blessed Virgin," p. 26).

Father Raymond E. Brown, one of the leading Catholic biblical scholars, says of her: "According to the criterion of discipleship based on doing the will of God,

Lucan Mary becomes the first Christian disciple" (*America*, May 15, 1982, p. 376).

In the Gospels there are various kinds of disciples. Peter, for example, is a prototype for apostle-disciples; the other eleven disciples or apostles are models for community discipleship. Mary, the Mother of Jesus, however, is a prototype for the believer-disciple, offering us an insight into our own discipleship in how to follow (*akolouthein*) Jesus.

Mark who is the first to produce a writing called a Gospel gives us but a trace of Mary and her discipleship. I like to see his presentation of her as a silhouette, for only the contours of her face and person are suggested. Though other images could be used, I applied those of an artist; each evangelist writer, so to speak, develops portraits of the people he describes through his words about them and from the context in which he places both the words and deeds of Jesus and those who surround or follow him.

Matthew, besides relying on the texts of Mark, develops his own sketch of Mary in his initial chapters. She is seen within the fulfillment theme that is characteristic of Matthew.

In the pages of Luke, Mary is the first faithful disciple of Jesus. She is with him from his conception (1:32–38); she is, of course, present as his Mother at his birth (2:6–7); as Mother and as the spouse of Joseph we see her with him in the presentation in the temple fulfilling all that is required of parents by the law (2:22–23). With Joseph her husband Mary finds Jesus the young adult among the learned doctors, listening to them and asking them questions. She is with Jesus all the time of the hidden life and probably remains with him as a widow when Joseph disappears from the pages of the Scriptures. Later on in Jesus' public life, a woman declares her a truly blessed person because of her Son, but Jesus affirms: "Still more blessed are those who hear the word of God and keep it" (11:27–28). This is said in her favor by Jesus because Luke already has informed us through Elizabeth that Mary is blessed because she believed that the promise made to her by the Lord would be fulfilled (1:45). Just as Mary bridged the infancy of Jesus to his youth, then his hidden life to his public, so too she is the only one who bridges his total life to a new birth in the Christian community when she is with the apostle-disciples and the brothers of Jesus and the women (Acts 1:14).

In the Gospel of John, we see her as a "single parent" at the wedding feast of Cana. Through her social sensitivity and her motherly concern, the party becomes a success (2:10). At Calvary she stands beneath the Cross while Jesus entrusts her to the beloved disciple (19:27).

All of us are able to identify with these specific aspects of her discipleship. She is not someone on a pedestal, but rather a believing woman disciple of Jesus who summons us to a creative following of Jesus as she did. Mary develops as a believing disciple of Jesus, that is, as a strong person of faith. Her limitations as a person who followed Jesus of Nazareth can help us to identify ourselves as disciples in the experiences of our life commitments.

Each of the four evangelists offers a distinct perspective on discipleship which has been shaped deliberately, according to the theology of the respective author.

In conclusion, as Catholics we might say that in Mary is summed up the longing and searching of the whole human race for God. She is the first who believes in Jesus Christ and the first to be saved from evil and death. She shows us the way of the true Christian life. Following the example of her faith, poverty of spirit, and attentiveness to the Lord, we hope to reflect to those around us Mary's warmth of welcome to God and to others. She cooperates with the Holy Spirit in setting free what is most tender, loving and vulnerable in a human being. Hence this book on Mary!

2

Mary, the Faithful Disciple of Jesus

These reflections of Mary are within the framework of the New Testament, the principal source for divine revelation throughout the past twenty centuries for us Christians. This biblical process of reflection consists in presenting Mary of Nazareth within the chronological scheme of the New Testament writings. In addition to developing the image of Mary through these texts, this book will also present her under a working paradigm which springs from the New Testament—the paradigm of discipleship. Mary will emerge as the first faithful disciple of Jesus. This theme grows from modest beginnings in the Pauline literature and develops through the four Gospels in a span of time roughly extending from 54 A.D. to 90–95 A.D. Chronologically in the Pauline literature (Galatians, Philippians, and Romans) we have merely a whisper, a shadow, or a dream-image of Mary. In Mark, the first evangelist, there is a silhouette of Mary as disciple. Matthew gives us a pencil sketch, so to speak, of the discipleship of Mary. In Luke, who is considered the artist of the New Testament Gospel, we have a portrait of Mary.

The fourth evangelist, John, presents her in sculpture through the two dramatic scenes of Cana and Calvary. The visionary scene of a woman clothed with the sun in the Apocalypse refers directly to the Church or the Christian community, yet it can be accommodated to Mary in the consummation of her call to discipleship.

The purpose of using discipleship for seeing Mary as the first faithful disciple is to provide a theme from which to survey the whole mystery of Mary as a person, as a believer, and as the first faithful disciple of the New Testament. Both her faith and her discipleship precede her motherhood; in fact, because of her faith is her motherhood possible. St. Augustine affirmed this in the fourth century when he said she first conceived Christ through faith before conceiving him in the flesh.

Father Patrick J. Bearsley, S.M., a Marian and biblical scholar, says that Mary as perfect disciple of Jesus offers to us a paradigm for our own discipleship. He offers a definition for the term "paradigm": a central thematic idea "rich and powerful enough to provide a vantage point from which to view all the other great truths about Mary" (Bearsley, *Theological Studies*, 1980, p. 469). This paradigm of Marian discipleship should help us to reflect more profoundly on the scriptural texts which refer to Mary whether directly or indirectly. With such a leading theme we can focus on her role as a believing disciple. All of her other titles and attributes given throughout the history of the Church would make better sense in the light of this biblical foundation of discipleship which is important for today's spirituality.

DISCIPLESHIP IN THE NEW TESTAMENT

In the Gospels we find that Jesus has given an original meaning to the term disciple (*mathetes*). With few exceptions, the term disciple is used in the New Testament solely for those who have recognized Jesus as their master or teacher. Thus we find that the "twelve" are first and foremost the disciples of Jesus:

> He summoned his twelve disciples, and gave them authority over unclean spirits with power to cast them out and to cure all kinds of diseases and sickness (Mt 12:1).

The disciples are those who form an intimate circle of friends who follow Jesus:

> If any man comes to me without hating his father, mother, wife, children, brothers, sisters, yes and his own life too, he cannot be my disciple. Anyone who does not carry his cross and come after me cannot be my disciple (Lk 14:26–27).

The seventy-two whom Jesus sent out on mission are also his disciples:

> After this the Lord appointed seventy-two others and sent them out ahead of him, in pairs, to all the towns and places he himself was to visit. He said to them, "The harvest is rich but the laborers are few, so ask the Lord of the harvest to send laborers to his harvest" (Lk 10:1–2).

In the Acts of the Apostles, after chapter six, it seems that every Christian is called a disciple. Luke tells us: "The word of the Lord continued to spread: the number of the disciples in Jerusalem was greatly increased, and a large group of priests made their submission to the faith" (cf. Acts 6:1; 6:7; 9:10–26).

Although Jesus has much in common with the rabbis and teachers of his time, he nevertheless does have special requirements for his own followers or disciples. First, there is the call (vocation) from Jesus himself independent of their moral or intellectual gifts. We have the calling of Simon Peter in Luke 5:8–11:

> When Simon Peter saw this he fell at the knees of Jesus saying, "Leave me, Lord. I am a sinful man." For he and all his companions were completely overcome by the catch they had made; so also were James and John, sons of Zebedee, who were Simon's partners. But Jesus said to Simon, "Do not be afraid; from now on it is men you will catch." Then, bringing their boats back to land, they left everything and followed him.

It is Jesus who initiates such a call. In many ways it is similar to our calling to a specific vocation (cf. Mk 1:17–20; Jn 1:38–50). The Father also is the one who has given these disciples to Jesus:

> Now the will of him who sent me is that I should lose nothing of all that he has given to me, and that I should raise it up on the last day (Jn 6:39).

> The Father who gave them to me is greater than anyone, and no one can steal from the Father. The Father and I are one (Jn 10:29–30; cf. Jn 17:6, 12).

Second, in the call to discipleship, there is a personal relationship and attachment to Jesus himself. The verb

15

"to follow" (*akolouthein*) is used to designate this intimacy with Jesus:

> One of the scribes then came up and said to him, "Master, I will follow you wherever you go." Jesus replied, "Foxes have holes and the birds of the air have nests, but the Son of Man has nowhere to lay his head." Another man, one of his disciples, said to him, "Sir, let me go and bury my father first." But Jesus replied, "Follow me, and leave the dead to bury their dead."

This close following of Jesus requires a complete break with one's past, a metanoia or conversion. When Jesus comes proclaiming the good news from God, he says:

> The time has come and the kingdom of God is close at hand. Repent (*metanoiete*) and believe the good news" (Mk 1:15; cf. Mt 4:17; Acts 2:38).

The Greek verb used above means to "think over," to "gain insight" into one's life and to change what needs to be changed. For sinners, changing one's mind or rethinking involves repenting or changing one's life; for religious people not conscious of sin the demand of *metanoien* might better be translated literally as a change of mind, attitude, or motivation. If one reflects on the opposition encountered by Jesus' demand, the Gospels record little rejection of him by sinners but quite the opposite from those who considered themselves right (cf. R.E. Brown, N.C.E.A., Keynote Address, April 22, 1981; Jn 9:40–41). To follow Jesus is to conform to his behavior, to listen to his teachings, and to imitate his life. In Mark 8:34–36, we read:

> He called the people and his disciples to him and said, "If anyone wants to be a follower of mine, let him re-

16

nounce himself and take up his cross and follow me. For anyone who wants to save his life will lose it; but anyone who loses his life for my sake, and for the sake of the gospel, will save it. What gain then is it for a man to win the whole world and ruin his life?" (cf. also Mk 10:21, 42–45; Jn 12:26).

Third, the disciples of Jesus have the same destiny and dignity as their Master, that is, they must carry their cross even daily (Lk 9:23), and drink the same cup of suffering that Jesus drinks (Mk 10:38), and, finally, receive from Jesus the gift of the kingdom (Mt 19:28f; Jn 14:3).

The theme of discipleship is concretely and clearly presented in the New Testament. It is a revealed way of following the plan of God through following Jesus Christ; it is not the fruit of later theological reflection, rather it springs immediately from the Gospel accounts and the words of Jesus. Since this concept of discipleship is common to all four evangelists and to St. Paul, Mary can emerge as a paradigm for discipleship in the early Christian communities, and our Catholic tradition about her can be better understood and shared once we are certain of her role in the New Testament.

Father Bearsley affirms:

By means of the perspective given by this paradigm, Mary's divine motherhood, her role in the Church, and the true significance of her virginity can be understood coherently as celebrations of the one total life experience which is the mystery of Mary in the plan of man's salvation (T.S., p. 472).

CHRONOLOGICAL OVERVIEW ON MARY'S DISCIPLESHIP

Chronologically, the earliest reference to Mary would spring from Mark's Gospel (3:31–35). This Gospel was finished by the year 70 A.D., when the temple in Jerusalem was destroyed by the Romans. The Gospel was probably written from a Galilean point of view for the converts to Christianity who came from that area. Some scholars feel that it was written at Rome, but had Galilean origins. We are fortunate to have parallels to this text of Mark in the other Synoptic Gospels: Matthew 12:46–50 and Luke 8:19–21. The fact that we have three Gospels recording a similar tradition, "multiple attestation," shows us that we are close to the earliest strata of information about the tradition of Mary and her relation to her Son Jesus.

Mark's pericope on Mary is presented in this way:

> His mother and his brothers arrived, and as they stood outside they sent word to him to come out. The crowd seated around him told him, "Your mother and your brothers and sisters are outside asking for you." He said in reply, "Who are my mother and my brothers?" And gazing around him at those seated in the circle he continued, "These are my mother and my brothers. Whoever does the will of God is brother and sister and mother to me" (Mk 1:31–35—N.A.B.).

Modern commentators are in agreement on the meaning of this passage. Father George Montague, S.M. describes the setting for this section as "The Spirit in Jesus—Jesus' New Family" (Mk 3:19–35). The author then describes the meaning of Mary's relationship to Jesus:

> Jesus' response means there is a relationship with him more real and important than the physical, especially when the latter impedes the inbreaking of the kingdom of God. In Jesus' new family of the spirit, rela-

tionship to him is established not by blood but by one's surrender to God's will revealed in Jesus . . . it is faith, not the flesh, that gives entry to the kingdom. And it is faith, obedient faith, that brings one into the new family and makes one brother and sister and mother to Jesus" (*Mark*, p. 50).

The final line, verse 35, tells us who truly constitute the family of Jesus from his point of view: it consists of those who do the will of God. Though Jesus seems to be excluding his natural family, he is not. He is, in a typical semitic manner, emphasizing what is his priority while drastically offsetting it with the natural ties of family. Later Mark will express the meaning of such discipleship when he says:

> Jesus answered: "I give you my word there is no one who has given up home, brothers or sisters, mother or father, children or property, for me and for the gospel who will not receive in this present age a hundred times as many homes, brothers and sisters, mothers, children and property and persecution besides—and in the age to come, everlasting life" (Mk 10:29–30).

Mark's account was probably used by Matthew and Luke. However, their own accounts shade the meaning, presenting Mary in a more positive fashion. In Matthew we read:

> He was still addressing the crowds when his mother and his brothers appeared outside to speak with him. Someone said to him, "Your mother and your brothers are standing out there and they wish to speak to you." He said to the one who had told him, "Who is my mother? Who are my brothers?" Then, extending his hand toward his disciples, he said, "There are my

19

mother and my brothers. Whoever does the will of my heavenly Father is brother and sister and mother to me" (Mt 12:46–50).

Matthew has used certain words to indicate clearly his intention. In the more rudimentary presentation of Mark, Jesus points simply toward those around him, but Matthew explicitly says Jesus stretched out his hands above his *disciples* and says: "Behold my mother and my brothers, for whoever *does the will of my heavenly Father*, that one is my brother and sister and mother." Matthew has omitted the shocking statement that Jesus' relatives thought he was insane. "When his family heard of this, they came to take charge of him, saying, 'He is out of his mind' " (Mk 3:21). He has also avoided Mark's generalization that all those seated about Jesus are his disciples. They are at best but potential believers. Those who have left their homes and families for the sake of Jesus (Mt 8:22; 10:37) are his real mother and brothers. Father John Meier in his *New Testament Message* on Matthew says:

> What Jesus asked of his disciples—the breaking of family ties—he himself now undertakes. *For blood ties count for nothing in the kingdom* (Mt 3:9). *What counts is being a disciple,* which Jesus goes on to define in terms of doing the will of "my Father" (N.T.M., p. 140).

Matthew is concerned about the community of believers remaining united. For him the Church is the family of God which is united through its baptism and its teacher, Jesus. The last paragraph of his Gospel is a key for interpreting the entire message of Jesus' words and works in Matthew:

> Jesus came up and spoke to them. He said, "All authority in heaven and on earth has been given to me.

20

Go, therefore, make disciples of all the nations; baptize them in the name of the Father and of the Son and of the Holy Spirit, and teach them to observe all the commands I gave you. And know that I am with you always; yes, to the end of time" (Mt 28:18–20).

Discipleship is a part of Matthew's message. In his community there is a danger of a split among those who are Gentile and those who are Jewish disciples. He, therefore, writes his Gospel by focusing on Jesus as their teacher while all are to be his disciples. Jesus, who is called Emmanuel only in this Gospel, is the visible presence of God with his people. As we have seen, he ends his Gospel with this thought and ties the beginning to the conclusion with the same theme in community prayer:

I tell you solemnly once again, if two of you on earth agree to ask anything at all, it will be granted to you by my Father in heaven. For where two or three meet in my name, I shall be there with them (Mt 18:18–20).

In carefully reading this Gospel and the other three we will come to see Jesus as one who never teaches or asks something of us without doing or accomplishing it himself. Unlike other rabbis or masters, he goes beyond what is expected of him and becomes a unique person who calls his disciples to a special manner of following him closely.

Luke, the final Synoptic evangelist also has a passage which is based on Mark's text:

His mother and brothers came to be with him, but they could not reach him because of the crowd. He was told, "Your mother and your brothers are standing outside and they wish to see you." He told them in reply, "My mother and my brothers are those who hear the word of God and act upon it" (Lk 8:19—21).

21

Luke is removed even farther from the death of Jesus than Matthew and Mark. Writing his double work called "Luke-Acts" around 85 A.D. he, too, reflects on the same tradition about Jesus and his family, but situates the account in a context which is forthright, positive—as is always the case—toward Mary, the Mother of Jesus. This incident is placed immediately after Luke's parable of the sower and the saying about light. In such a meeting, Luke has Jesus indicating that "truly hearing the word of God included doing that word and that those who both heard and did the word were Jesus' true family" (cf. N.T.M., LaVerdiere, p. 114).

Luke enlarges the notion of discipleship to challenge the followers of Jesus in their mission. Discipleship in this Gospel is an apostolic call to do and to teach as Jesus did.

Luke presents Mary within this theme of discipleship while avoiding any kind of rejection of Mary on the part of Jesus. It could well be that Mary had a more prominent role in the Lukan community than in the ecclesial communities of Mark and Matthew. Luke has thus softened the harsher image of Mark and personalized the more structured message of Matthew about Mary. All three accounts are inspired, but Luke's is the most developed in appreciating the role of Mary as disciple.

We can summarize what has been said by Father Bearsley's insightful remarks about these passages:

The import of these passages cannot be mistaken. In Jesus' estimation, discipleship is more important than family relationships. But the incident as related by Mark and Matthew seems to imply also a rejection of his mother and relatives in favor of his "family" of disciples. In R. Brown's judgment, "clearly he is replacing his natural family with a family of believers, those who will do the will of God." What is clear is that Mark and Matthew did not intend in their narration of this incident to have as its primary meaning Jesus' rejection of his mother and family. . . . Rather, *their primary intention may have been simply to convey the primacy of discipleship* as forcefully as possible, and the idiom used had the unfortunate side-effect of suggesting a snubbing of Mary on the part of Jesus, which was not intended (T.S., pp. 474–475).

Matthew and Luke are the first interpreters of Mark. In seeing how they have described Mary's relationship with Jesus, we notice they have not read a negative intention in Mark's mentioning of Mary. They are faithful to a living tradition they have received and have handed it on to their communities through their respective Gospels. Had they not done so positively, the tradition of Mary would have been vitiated from the beginning, but as they demonstrate by their accounts of this incident, there was no rejection of Mary at the heart of the tradition they received and faithfully passed on to their communities and to us.

MARY, DISCIPLE AND WOMAN OF FAITH

In calling Mary a disciple we are also speaking of her as a woman of faith. If one asks what Mary did to conceive Jesus, the answer is simply: she made an act of faith. And then the Word was made flesh (Jn 1:14). Mary's faith as a disciple was the reason for her motherhood. She heard the word of God and responded to it, kept it, pondered it over in her heart (Lk 2:19, 51). Father Bearsley comments, "Her conceiving of Christ was from her point of view first and foremost a faith-event, and it is in viewing her as a dis-

23

ciple that her role in the Incarnation makes the most sense" (p. 480).

If her motherhood has been overemphasized, through biblical studies it can be better explained and understood by us. She gives us hope as a young woman who is receptive to God's invitation at the Annunciation: she hears from Gabriel that nothing is impossible to God; she responds in faith: "I am the handmaid of the Lord; let what you have said be done to me" (Lk 1:38). Her discipleship is beginning on this grace-filled occasion. It will continue to grow as she learns the cost of discipleship in following Jesus, the challenge of it as he becomes hated and persecuted, and perfected as he dies upon the cross while confiding one disciple, Mary his Mother, to the beloved disciple (Jn 19:25–28a).

It is from the Book of Signs or the first part of John's Gospel (chapters one through twelve) that the theme of faith is constantly presented and developed by the fourth evangelist. In the first seven signs of faith in this first part of John, Mary is present at Cana. Through her belief in the person of her Son, Jesus, and his power, the first of his great signs is accomplished. She was among the disciples of Jesus of whom it is said at the end of this narrative: "He let his glory be seen and his disciples believed in him" (Jn 1:12).

In summary, the Scriptures present Mary as a disciple in an ever-growing and maturing sense. We will see this as we progress chronologically through the New Testament to see what it says about her. She, too, like her Son, grows in wisdom, age, and grace as the years pass. Her discipleship, like ours, is a normal, dynamic growth in the coming to know, love, and follow her Son, Jesus. She is a woman of faith who can be emulated; she is not an unreachable ideal woman on a pedestal.

3

Mary in the Pauline Writings

The earliest writings in the New Testament stem from St. Paul. We are certain that his letters occurred between 50 A.D. and 60 A.D., probably ten to fifteen years before Mark wrote the first Gospel. In his Epistles Paul gives us but an echo, a whisper, a shadow of Mary. We come to know more of her Judaic background and that of her Son through Paul than anything historical about her. Yet, what he says is important, even though it is but a trace of evidence about her. We are puzzled at the fact that Paul records no words of Jesus and relatively little about Jesus' life since he was the most effective apostle-disciple and preacher of Jesus Christ in the nascent Christian Church. Undoubtedly, as a brilliant Jew versed in the methods of the rabbis, he was aware of the oral traditions about the man Jesus, but because of the pressing needs and concerns of the apostolic churches, he was more of a pastor than a recording evangelist, more of a preacher who traveled from village to city to highland to bring the simple message to all Gentiles, "Jesus is Lord."

Paul's spirituality is Christ-centered. He uses the expression "in Christ" over one hundred and fifty times.

The mystery of Christ's suffering, death, and especially his resurrection, is central in Paul's response to the Lord and in the call to holiness for all the Christians of his churches. He never uses the word disciple nor does he speak of discipleship. How then can we see Mary as a disciple in the Pauline literature? Certainly Mary is not directly spoken of in his writings, but we can see that as a Jewish woman she, too, was totally immersed "in Christ," her Son and her Lord. As a faithful believer she meets Paul's criterion for holiness, namely, to be centered in Christ and his mysteries through faith.

Paul, unlike the evangelists, was not interested in the earthly history and ministry of Jesus. In fact in 2 Corinthians 5:16 he says: ". . . henceforth we know no one according to the flesh. And even though we have known Christ according to the flesh, yet now we know him so no longer." His own concern was that all believers be imitators of Jesus Christ even as Paul was:

> Remain united, becoming imitators of me, brothers;
> and keep your eye on those who live according to the
> example you have in us (Phil 3:17).

And in 1 Corinthians 11:1 he clearly says:

> Become imitators of me, just as I am an imitator of
> Christ.

Paul's first Epistle is to the Thessalonians, probably written in 51 A.D., while his last treatise could be that of Romans, written around the year 58 A.D. Thus the earliest writing of the Christians takes place a generation after the death of Jesus. Within these letters of Paul there are formulations and belief-statements which come to Paul from other believers. Some of these, like the famous

26

Christ hymn of Philippians (cf. Phil 2:6–11), could have existed a decade before Paul actually wrote. Any implicit and remote considerations that we have about Mary within the group of Pauline writings are limited to the following texts: Galatians 1:19; 4:4–5; and 4:28–29; Romans 1:3–4; and Philippians 2:6–7. Thus the echo of Mary is reduced to nine lines within Paul's Epistles, and all of these references are faint and implicit at best.

1. *Philippians 2:6–7*

> Though he was in the form of God, he did not deem equality with God something to be grasped at. Rather he emptied himself and took on the form of a slave (*doulou*), being born in the likeness of men.

The Epistle to the Philippians is well known to us through the liturgical responses of Holy Week. It is the most ancient of Christological hymns, and still is a treasured passage for most Christians. Often it is called the "Carmen Christi"—the Hymn about the Christ. This poem was probably derived from a pre-Pauline liturgical setting and was known to Paul and his readers:

> Though he (Jesus) was in the form of God,
> he emptied himself,
> taking the form of a servant
> being born in the likeness of men (Phil 2:7).

The New American Bible (Catholic) infers by the parallel passages it gives that these verses speak in a similar way to the Prologue of John's Gospel (Jn 1:11), and have resonances of John 17:5 and Hebrews 1:3. Exegetes and theologians speak of the "pre-existence" of the Word of God through these lines of the inspired text. If that be the case, then we have an exalted image of Jesus in Paul, or what the theologians call a "high Christology." Such passages led to formulations on the Trinity in the third and fourth centuries. If, too, as scholars state, this hymn flows from a liturgical setting, then we also come to realize that some of the most profound and lofty statements about Jesus come to us through early liturgical worship. On the other hand, there are scholars who maintain the hymn does not speak of a pre-existent Person or Logos.

The Marian implication is seen in the above verse where the "emptying-out" and the "being born" are referred to in the person of Jesus, the Christ. The word for "birth" (*ginesthai*) and the word for servant (*doulos*) are the echo of a Marian implication here. We must remember that Paul leads into the hymn with the words: "Have this mind among yourselves, which you have in Christ Jesus" (Phil 2:5). The thought can mean: this person who now is God-man has totally emptied himself in becoming human and has taken on the condition of a slave or servant by assuming human nature. Jesus took his human nature from his Mother, Mary. Like her who called herself the "handmaid" (*doule* is used in Luke 1:48 in her hymn) of the Lord, this hymn calls Christ the *doulos* or servant. The "emptying out" of Jesus is complemented by the humility, openness, and poverty of Mary who totally emptied herself out to God to be filled with his word. God in the person of Jesus emptied himself to take on the characteristics of a servant by being born of a Jewish woman, Mary of Nazareth. These written words of an ancient hymn echo a thin trace of the presence of Mary. We have to remember the tradition that Luke was a companion of Paul. The expression of verse 7 is evocative of Mary's Magnificat in Luke's Gospel. Perhaps the ideas of both hymns are parallel. The characteristics of a faithful dis-

28

ciple are present in both the Christ whom Paul is praising and in Mary who is totally dependent on God. She is one of the poor of Yahweh (*anawim*) who are referred to in the Psalms and who trust so magnanimously in God. Her obedience and humility are the other dispositions that are so similar to those expressed in the Pauline use of the hymn.

In the same verse, the word "being born" can only factually be understood of the woman who brought forth the Christ. Paul may not know or say anything about the virginity of Mary; likewise he never says anything against it. We will come close to the same idea in Paul's own reflection in Galatians 4:4.

2. *Romans 1:3–4*

The second Pauline reference which is of interest to us is that of the Epistle to the Romans 1:3–4:

> The gospel concerning his Son, who was descended from David according to the flesh and designated Son of God in power according to the Spirit of holiness by his resurrection from the dead, Jesus Christ our Lord.

In this passage we have the earliest reference to Jesus as the promised Messiah who was born of the Davidic seed according to the flesh in his human existence. The lines can be paralleled with one another to show us the humanness of Jesus which springs from Mary his Mother, and the graced-nature of the Christ who belongs to God:

Humanness:	**Divine likeness:**
the Messiah was *born* (of Mary)	and was made or designated
from the seed of David (through Joseph and Mary?)	Son of God in power

according to the flesh (again Mary)	according to the Spirit of holiness as of the resurrection of the dead

Biblical scholars assert that Paul is using a kerygmatic statement or proclamation about who Jesus is: this statement was already in use among those Christians before Paul knew them. Paul wittingly makes use of this credal statement in the introduction of this Epistle to express relationship by human descent or kinship in the Davidic Messianic line. We are at least certain of the parenting of Mary; Paul is not interested in her virginity; but, then again, he gives no evidence about a human father of Jesus. In chapter nine he returns to the ancestry of the Christ:

> For I could wish that I myself were accursed and cut off from Christ for the sake of my brethren, my kinsmen by race. . . . To them belong the patriarchs, *and of their race, according to the flesh, is the Christ.* God who is over all be blessed for ever. Amen (Rom 9:3, 5).

We note that Paul is only interested in the Messiah, that is, the Christ, and not in his parents. But the fact that he does mention the Davidic descendance leads us to think of Mary and Joseph especially through what we know from Matthew 1:18–25. The concepts of the human origins of the Messiah have always been expressed in the Christian understanding of the Messiah.

There are several Catholic scholars who would see an indication of Mary's virginity in Paul's use of the verb "to be born of" which is found in several passages (Rom 1:3; Phil 2:7; Gal 4:4). In the form that Paul uses there is evidence that this verb *(ginesthai)* means to "come into being." Had Paul wanted to stress the fact that Jesus was born of a human father he would have used another verb which clearly means to be begotten by a human father, namely, *gennasthai.*

Father Joseph Fitzmyer, S.J., however, has the better interpretation in seeing the text more in reference to the resurrection of Jesus than to the manner of his human birth. Fitzmyer says:

> Paul's real goal in the parallelism of Romans 1:3–4 is not so much to connect Jesus with the Davidic line as to affirm that Jesus, the Davidic Messiah, is risen. To read more into the use of the verb "ginesthai" in Rom. 1:3 or for that matter in Gal. 4:4 or in Phil. 2:7 is over-interpretation and is close to eisegesis (*Mary in the New Testament,* p. 38).

Thus in this pre-Pauline formula Jesus is designated Son of God in power through the resurrection. Such Scripture is the beginning of a trajectory of thought resulting in later Christian formulations about the human and divine natures in Christ, especially in the Councils of Nicea in 325 A.D. and Ephesus in 431 A.D. The contrast of the phrase that Paul presents shows us that Jesus "according to the flesh" is related to humanity through the Davidic line, whereas Jesus as "designated according to the Spirit" is related to the power of God who raises him from the dead. Unlike Luke, Paul never uses the word "Spirit" to refer to the active power of God in the conception of Jesus (cf. Lk 1:32, 35; Mt 1:20). In Luke it is from the action of the Spirit that the virginity of Mary is rendered fruitful.

3. *Galatians 1:19*

The final writing of Paul which has some bearing on the person of Mary is the Epistle to the Galatians. The three passages which have a Marian import are Galatians 1:19, 4:4, and 4:28–29. Paul writes in Galatians: "But I saw none of the other apostles except James the Lord's brother" (Gal 1:19). This issue is raised in Mark where the "brothers" of Jesus are mentioned. Is this James a blood-brother of Jesus and a child of Mary? In the language that Paul used this is a possibility, for James is described as the *ton adelphon tou Kyriou*—the brother of the Lord. This text is similar to the Marian reference which reads: "Is not this the carpenter, the son of Mary and brother of James and Joses and Judas and Simon, and are not his sisters here with us?" (Mk 6:3). These texts are important, for they could be saying something about Mary that is not affirmed in the Catholic tradition. They are also texts which could mean "brother" and "sister" in an extended sense and not literally a blood-brother of Jesus whose mother is Mary. An interesting exercise for the reader could be to contrast what the Catholic edition of a New Testament says about these verses with respect to what may be said in other versions. For example, the Oxford Annotated Bible, that is, the Revised Standard Version, has this footnote for Galatians 1:19: "James, the Lord's brother, the younger son of Mary the wife of Joseph (see Mt 13:55n; Mk 6:3n)." The statement is simply affirmed without any explanation. We will come to see that the issue is not that simple when we return to the question in Mark's Gospel (3:31–35) and the meaning of the brothers and sisters of Jesus. On the other hand, the Jerusalem Bible, a Catholic version, says: "but only James . . . others translate 'except James,' either identifying this James with the son of Alpheus, Mt 10:3, and taking him for one of the Twelve, or else understanding apostle in the wider sense; cf. Rom. 1:1." What we see is that the different

Christian dispensations interpret these texts according to their tradition and piety.

4. *Galatians 4:4*

> But when the designated time (*chronos*) had come, God sent forth his Son born of a woman, born under the law, to deliver from the law those who were subjected to it, so that we might receive our status as adopted sons (Gal 4:4–5).

This text of Galatians 4:4 is within the section of the epistle which refers to the true sons (and daughters) of Abraham (Gal 4:1–31). I have added verse five to complete the meaning of Paul's thought which shows that those formerly under the law become free of its burdensome regulations and become the adopted sons (and daughters) of God in Christ. The sense of the section is that Jesus' birth in history is a salvific event which enables all, both Jew and Gentile, to be true offspring and heirs of the inheritance promised to Abraham. Paul throughout this letter is speaking of our justification by faith alone and not by observance of the Mosaic prescriptions. (There were 613 distinct observations for the Pharisaic Jew.)

Paul has built up his arguments for this section by basing his comparison of freedom from servitude through belief in Christ. This is similar to a child who finally has become an adult and is no longer under the tutelage of a custodian. The heritage now is enjoyed. The history of salvation from Abraham to Moses was the time of humankind's juvenile condition; full maturity comes with the birth of freedom in and through Jesus Christ who is the center of salvation history. The Christ-event (Jesus' life, death, and resurrection) has enabled us to be heirs as sons and daughters. Paul says: "So through God you are no longer a *slave* but a *son* (and *daughter*), and if a *son* (and *daughter*) then an heir" (v. 7). Paul is convinced that true sonship and daughterhood are assured by God's fidelity to the promise made to Abraham now fully realized through Jesus Christ.

Paul's statement that Jesus "was born of a woman" (whom we know to be Mary through the Gospels) is the most explicit statement about the Mother of Jesus in his writings. Because Jesus is born of this Jewish woman, circumcision is mandatory. The woman (Mary) and her child submit to this Mosaic law.

Jesus' submission to the total human condition, to the demands of his culture and religion enables him to fulfill the law's purpose and bring it to a conclusion (Gal 3:19–25). Later, in Matthew's Gospel, Jesus himself states: "Do not think that I have come to abolish the law and the prophets. I have come, not to abolish them, but to fulfill them. Of this much I assure you: until heaven and earth pass away, not the smallest letter of the law, not the smallest part of a letter, shall be done away with until it all comes true" (Mt 5:17–18). Paul affirms that the law was time-bound until the offspring to whom the promise was made was born. Once Jesus was born in the fullness of time, then the era of salvation and freedom from the law was ushered into human history and destiny.

In Galatians 4:4 Paul demonstrates the reality of Jesus' humanity by the Hebrew expression "one born of a woman"; he shows Jesus' Jewishness and his belonging to that community by saying, "one born under the law." The former expression is amply attested to in the scriptures (Jb 14:1; 15:14; 25:4; Mt 11:11; Lk 7:28 and also in the Dead

Sea Scrolls). The latter expression refers to Jesus' circumcision, but implicitly; Paul does not want to give in to the opposing Judaizers in the Galatian community.

Modern scholars see in this passage another pre-Pauline credal formula similar to that of Philippians 2:6–7. Since the words "born under the law to redeem those under the law" is Paul's own contestation against the Judaizers, the following formula remains:

> God sent forth his Son (born of a woman) that we might receive adoption as sons.

This credal sentence is the forerunner of what the Nicene Creed would declare: "Who for our sake became man and was born of the Virgin Mary." Paul's reference to Mary, however, is a remote one. She is simply the woman who brought him into the world. There is no hint of a miraculous birth nor even that he was a first-born of this woman. But what Paul says about Jesus as the Christ is not at all incompatible with statements about Jesus in Matthew and Luke who do affirm a virginal conception in their introductory chapters.

Father Fitzmyer gives us a clear interpretation:

> Such a description simply stresses the *human condition* of Jesus. I would be reluctant to draw from the verse the virginal conception either from Paul's use of "beget" or from the absence of the mention of any father. For scriptural evidence of the virginity of Mary we must turn to Matthew and Luke. Seemingly Paul was simply making use of a stereotyped literary expression and was not attempting to supply detail on *how* the Son became man" (*Mary in the New Testament*, p. 43).

5. *Galatians 4:28–29*

> Now we brethren, like Isaac, are children of the promise. But as at that time he who was born according to the flesh persecuted him who was born according to the Spirit, so it is now.

This last text selected from Paul parallels the section of Galatians 4:1–11 which can be summarized under the title "slaves versus sons." Section 4:21–31 is also similar in title: "Sons of the slave girl versus sons of the freeborn wife (4:21–31)" (*Seven Pauline Letters*, Peter F. Ellis, Liturgical Press, Minnesota, p. 176). Paul captures his Jewish Christian audience with a colorful rabbinic allegory of Sarah and Isaac, the son of promise, and Hagar, the slave woman, who gives birth to Ishmael, a son "of the flesh" (*kata sarka*). Sarah represents those who are free of the law through faith; her son, Isaac, the child born from God's promise, is a symbol of Jesus, while Hagar represents those bound to the law and her son, Ishmael, the slave-born son dependent on the law.

In the allegory Paul uses, Isaac and Jesus are the "sons of the one born free" (Gal 4:30). Isaac is the child "born according to the Spirit" (Gal 4:29)—because of the faith of Abraham—and Jesus, too, is the child born according to the Spirit because of Mary's faith. Is Paul implying that Isaac was conceived through the activity of the Spirit without a human father? According to Palestinian conservative rabbinic Judaism, it is God who helps Abraham and Sarah to have a son and this is more in keeping with the Hebrew text of Genesis 21:1–14. Yet, Paul was strongly influenced by Philo and Hellenistic Judaism which has this interpretation about Sarah's conception:

The Lord visited Sarah as he had said, and the Lord did
to Sarah as he had promised.

This interpretation could have influenced Paul when he
reflected on the passage of Genesis he uses to compare
with our own adoption as sons and daughters of God in
Galatians.

In summarizing the relationship of Jesus to his
mother Mary in the Pauline writings, we can see that
there is only a whisper of her presence and her discipleship. She is the *woman* of whom he is born into the history of salvation. From her his humanness and similarity
to us in all things except sin is inferred (2 Cor 5:21). His
existence in the Palestinian Jewish community as a Jew
depends upon his being born of this Jewish woman. Paul
did not even whisper her name!

Mary in Mark's Gospel

Discipleship Texts: Mark 2:13–17; 8:31–35; 9:30–32; 10:32–45
Mary Texts: Mark 3:31–35; 6:1–6a

Mark's is the earliest written Gospel, and the first Christian writing that deserves the name of Gospel, that is, "good news." It was written during 65–70 A.D. Mark develops the theme of discipleship while calling the believing Christian community to overcome any of its selfish attachments so that the believers may become followers of Jesus Christ. His Gospel presents the disturbing call of the cost of discipleship.

The powerful symbol of the lion is used for Mark in the tradition of Christian art. Mark's Gospel is a challenging and ferocious bellow to follow Jesus despite the overwhelming oppression from those who hate the Christian community. We must remember that one strong tradition associates Rome as the place of origin for this Gospel; the madman Nero was reigning at the time this Gospel was being formed. We are, therefore, not too far removed from the time when Christians were also being thrown to the lions. A reminiscence of such an era of persecution may be the background of Mark's statement:

He stayed in the wasteland forty days, put to the test there by Satan. He was with the *wild beasts,* and angels waited on him (Mk 1:13).

More recent scholarship, without removing the threat of violent persecution, posits the idea that this Gospel was written for the Galilean Christians who eventually fled to Pella across the Jordan because of the Roman legions. These Jewish-Christians thereby became estranged from their fellow-Jewish neighbors while giving up their homeland and Jewish heritage.

Mark is a colorful and energetic writer as well. His pages are replete with details; he is the J.D. Salinger of the New Testament writers. The invigorating youthful flavor of the Galilean traditions come through his accounts of Jesus and his disciples. For those who favor the influence of St. Peter on this Gospel, there is the saying of an early writer, Papias of Hierapolis:

And the presbyter said this: Mark became the interpreter of Peter and wrote down accurately all that he remembered without, however, recording in order the things said or done by the Lord. For he had not heard the Lord, nor had he followed him, but afterwards, as I said, followed Peter, who used to give instructions as necessity demanded but had no design of giving an arrangement of the Lord's oracles, so that Mark made no mistake in thus writing down single points as he remembered them. For he made it his one care to leave out nothing of what he had heard and to make no false statement in them (Eusebius, *Church History,* 3, 39, 15–16).

The apostle Peter came from Capernaum in Galilee (Mk 1:16–22, 29–31). The tradition that Mark was his follower can account for the Galilean origins of this Gospel.

Mark's Gospel probably was written some thirty-five to forty years after the death of Jesus. Most likely, 70 A.D. is the conjectured date because of his accurate description of his predicted fall of Jerusalem. Contemporary scholarly opinion has the Gospel issuing from Galilee, or a more conservative hunch is that it emanated from Rome. Mark is an activist, a busybody who locates the facts and embellishes them with his descriptive technique. He is sensate and judgmental; he is strong in feeling. He is also the most practical-minded of the four evangelists.

As a Gospel writer Mark needs to complete the picture; that is what Matthew and Luke do for him. He needs to integrate the traditions about Jesus' words and deeds in order to balance them better. He needs to mellow and mature. The later evangelists, realizing these deficiencies, would use his material, but add and improve upon it to complete their narrative of the Jesus story. The final evangelist, John, used Mark's Gospel sparingly while Matthew uses over ninety percent of Markan texts and Luke over thirty percent.

In Mark's Gospel there are only two chapters in which Mary is presented (3:31–35; and 6:1–6a). It is only in chapter 3:31–35 where Mary actually appears within a scene. In chapter 6:1–6 she is only mentioned. There are three other verses in which the name Mary appears, but in all probability this is not Mary, the Mother of Jesus. Only a few scholars think she is named in these texts (15:40, 47; 16:1). It is from Mark's basic outline of the baptism of Jesus, his active ministry in Galilee, his journey to Jerusalem with the ensuing suffering and death, and finally the hint at his resurrection that the other Synoptic evangelists, Luke and Matthew, have a literary basis and source for their gospels.

Our interest in seeing Mary as a first disciple within

the pages of each Gospel makes it necessary to trace the theme of discipleship in Mark. The redactional method of studying the texts helps us to see the notion of discipleship in the total context and within the community experience of each particular Gospel. The method likewise is concerned with attempting to rediscover each evangelist's intention. Through this method Mark is seen as a person directing the traditional material he has gathered towards certain of his own theological and communitarian interests. A Gospel is not a literal history of Jesus and his words and deeds, but rather a directed gathering into written form of the oral traditions and of the sayings of Jesus which come from the memory of the Markan community. Without going into details, the background and understanding of the Markan community should help us to present discipleship from his perspective. Naturally, Mary would be seen within such a perception.

The recent Markan scholarship has posited discipleship in this Gospel as a paradox and a costly challenge. All of Jesus' disciples fall short of their discipleship. Though they misunderstand, fail, and obstruct such a call, they nevertheless are important witnesses for Mark's community. Perhaps their disappointing failures are presented so glaringly that the Christian community of Mark may avoid what they have done. The Markan community should be confident in its call while remaining faithful despite opposition, persecution, and separation from the homeland and the physical presence of Jesus who came from Galilean territory.

In Mark's Gospel the disciples falter and never sustain their faith response to Jesus. Only the demons and the so-called outsiders seem to confess Jesus. In fact, the climax of the Gospel is the centurion's declaration, "Truly, this was the son of God" (Mk 15:39). Peter, mo-

41

ments after his profession of faith in Jesus, weakens and refuses to understand what it really means to follow Jesus in his suffering and death at the hands of his own people's leaders. So, too, the rest of the disciples fail Jesus on numerous occasions, such as after the multiplication of the loaves and fishes:

> They had forgotten to bring any bread along; except for one loaf they had none with them in the boat. So when he instructed them, "Keep your eyes open! Be on your guard against the yeast of the Pharisees and the yeast of Herod," they concluded among themselves that it was because they had no bread. Aware of this he said to them, "Why do you suppose that it is because you have no bread? Do you still not see or comprehend? Are your minds completely blinded? Have you eyes but no sight? Ears but no hearing? Do you remember when I broke the five loaves for the five thousand, how many baskets of fragments you gathered up?" They answered, "Twelve." "When I broke the seven loaves for the four thousand how many full hampers of fragments did you collect?" They answered, "Seven." He said to them again, "Do you still not understand?" (Mk 8:14–21).

The relatives and immediate family of Jesus are also in consternation over Jesus and his activity in Galilee. They are concerned about his behavior and how he is not conforming to their expectations. To comprehend Mary's role in Mark's Gospel the section from chapter three, verse twenty, must form the background for discerning who she is in relationship to Jesus. In this scene, his brothers and family relatives are searching for him because they consider him to be beside himself. Their own simple family reputation is at stake; they seek Jesus to take him away from his disturbing activities and speech in the areas surrounding his home town. Mary appears among them as a Jewish mother concerned about her son and her own family reputation. The Markan sketch of her is so rapid and thin that all we have is a silhouette of her, that of a Jewish woman called Mary, the Mother of Jesus. Mark centers exclusively on Jesus, but identifies him as "the son of Mary" (Mk 6:3). Is it that she, too, doesn't comprehend the secret of her Son Jesus? Is this another hint at what we call the Messianic secret in Mark by means of the expression "son of Mary"? What does this stark picture of Mary tell us about her own relationship to Jesus? Is she, too, a typical disciple of Jesus who misunderstands his deeper message and meaning in life?

At most in Mark she is his Mother, Mary of Nazareth. Mark's reflections on the family of Jesus are probably reflections based on Galilean traditions which could ultimately spring from his own relatives. The beginnings of the relationship as Mark records them are rugged in their simplicity, but they will enable others to build upon that same tradition with literary, theological, and creative freedom. In Mark there is more unsaid than said.

> His mother and his brothers arrived, and as they stood outside they sent word to him to come out. The crowd seated around him told him, "Your mother and your brothers and sisters are outside asking for you." He said in reply, "Who are my mother and my brothers?" And gazing around him at those seated in the circle he continued, "These are my mother and my brothers. Whoever does the will of God is brother and sister and mother to me" (Mk 3:31–35).

We can only make some sense out of Mary's presence in this scene if we see it in terms of *discipleship* and *family*.

43

She appears within the active ministry of Jesus in Galilee in search of him. The purpose of this pericope is within the larger theme and context of a call to discipleship. From the outer circle of disbelief and scandal because of Jesus there is the call to discipleship in the inner circle of those who believe in him. Those seated around Jesus are considered his true followers because they are listening to him. They who do the will of the Father are the brothers and sisters and mother. They constitute the true family of Jesus. Mark through these verses could also be encouraging his own community to reflect on their relationship to Jesus in a response of faith and fidelity to the will of the Father.

In tracing back this tradition about Jesus and his human family, the form-critical scholars are convinced we have an important saying of Jesus: "Behold my mother and my brothers! Whoever does the will of God is my brother, and sister, and mother." This dictum would relate to those believing disciples who truly form the kingdom of God on earth as the true family of Jesus. The most recent group of scholars who studied this passage state: "This eschatological family (brother, sister, and mother) consists of those who do God's will" (*Mary in the New Testament*, p. 53). It would be this spiritual relationship that has importance for Jesus, not the physical natural ties of brother, sister and mother. Though this may not indicate a rejection of such ties on the part of Jesus, it does show us the priority of discipleship for those who listen and believe as the eschatological family of Jesus.

The second pericope of Mark (6:1–6a) presents the family of Jesus and calls us once more to put our full trust in him, unlike the response of his own neighbors—not attaching ourselves to the concerns of the family, but to the will of the Father. The passage reads:

He departed from there and returned to his own part of the country followed by his disciples. When the sabbath came he began to teach in the synagogue in a way that kept his large audience amazed. They said: "Where did he get all this? What kind of wisdom is he endowed with? How is it that such miraculous deeds are accomplished by his hands? Is this not the carpenter, the son of Mary, a brother of James and Joses and Judas and Simon? Are not his sisters our neighbors here?" They found him too much for them. Jesus' response to all this was: "No prophet is without honor except in his native place, among his own kindred, and in his own house." He could work no miracle there, apart from curing a few who were sick by laying hands on them, so much did their lack of faith distress him (Mk 6:1–6a).

The third verse identifies Jesus as the carpenter, the son of Mary. It then names James, Joses, Judas and Simon as his brothers. Are these also the children of Mary, his Mother? This text and the other texts which refer to the brothers or brother of Jesus and his sisters are important for a consideration of the fact of Mary's virginity which is presented in Matthew's and Luke's first chapters. As we have already seen in Galatians 1:19, Paul, too, referred to James as a brother of the Lord. The other New Testament passages which refer to the brothers of Jesus are found in the following texts: Mark 3:31–35; Matthew 12:46–50; Luke 8:19–21; Mark 6:3; Matthew 13:55–56; John 2:12; 7:3, 5, 10; Matthew 28:10; John 20:17; Galatians 1:19; 1 Corinthians 9:5; Acts 1:14.

All of these texts use the Greek word *adelphos* meaning brother. Ever since the third and fourth centuries, these texts have been interpreted in three distinct ways which are still accepted by the Christian Churches of to-

45

day. The mainstream religious positions of Catholicism, Anglicanism, and Protestantism generally propound one of these three ancient ways of interpretation. Only recently with efforts at studying the texts together ecumenically has some understanding of the others' tradition and opinion been achieved. No absolute solution can be reached from the texts themselves, but a history of the traditions has enabled Christians at least to understand where the other person is coming from in the interpretation.

Literally, the word *adelphos* means a blood-brother. But it is also on thirty different occasions in Acts a word which refers to the spiritual or Christian bond of fellowship or brotherhood. Paul uses it over one hundred and thirty times in his writings in this extended spiritual sense. Another important idea is that Hebrew and Aramaic use the word brother in the sense of a kinsman or relative, a cousin, a member of the same clan. Such an understanding prevails among the Arabs today and, in general, among the Africans.

The texts posed no problem for the first two centuries of Christianity, but a definite concern emerges in the Church during the third and fourth centuries. Tertullian, Helvidius, Jovinian and Bonosus interpret the text as saying that these are the brothers of Jesus and Mary is their mother. Origen and Epiphanius come up with another interpretation based on some of the apocryphal gospels (Protoevangelium of James, the Infancy Story of Thomas) which says that these brothers are half-brothers from Joseph the carpenter's former wife. St. Hilary of Poitiers and Ambrosiaster in the Western Church accepted this interpretation. St. Jerome's interpretation is the one favored by the Catholic tradition, for it maintains that all of the above references to the brothers and sisters of Jesus mean the cousins; thereby Mary's virginity is permanent.

These three interpretations can easily be discovered in commentaries today and an almost perfect reflection of the three traditions comes through: the Catholic commentators generally follow St. Jerome, the Anglican and Episcopalian have Epiphanius' opinion that the brothers and sisters are children of Joseph but not of Mary, whereas most Protestant commentators simply affirm that the texts literally mean the blood-brothers of Jesus. In the most definitive study among Catholic scholars, J. Blinzler summarizes his research:

> The so-called brothers and sisters of Jesus were male and female cousins. The relationship of Simon and Jude with Jesus occurs through their father Klopas and thus these were Davidides; their mother's name is unknown. The mother of the Lord's brothers, James and Joses, was a different Mary from the Lord's Mother. Either she or her husband was related to the family of Jesus, but the nature of this relationship cannot be ascertained (*Die Brüder und Schwestern Jesu*, p. 138).

More recently the conclusions of an ecumenical study of the question gave us the following four points:

1. The continued virginity of Mary after the birth of Jesus is not a question directly raised by the New Testament.
2. Once it was raised in subsequent Church history, it was that question which focused on the exact relationship of the "brothers" (and "sisters") of Jesus.

3. Once that attention has been focused, it cannot be said that the New Testament identifies them *without doubt* as blood brothers and sisters and hence as children of Mary.
4. The solution favored by scholars will in part depend on the authority they allot to later Church insights (*Mary in the New Testament,* p. 72).

In summary we can say that Mark's Gospel presents us with the cost of our discipleship. The example of the first disciples in Mark is one of failure. They are depicted more often as persons who misunderstand Jesus, as people filled with fear, lacking the courage to continue with Jesus. Mark tries to offset their fear, misunderstanding and failure.

Mark's image of Mary is a limited one. She is present in the first scene as a concerned parent who doesn't fathom who her Son is nor what he is about. Jesus, on the other hand, is calling his followers to true discipleship (Mk 3:31–35) which is not based on a blood relationship. Mary is present in the scene, but on the outside of the circle of listeners who surround Jesus. Her patient waiting and inquiry represent our own struggles in following Jesus. Struggling with our doubts, we come to a deeper faith and stronger commitment to Jesus. Such is the call of discipleship both for Mary and for us.

Mark challenges us when we feel we have only begun to find out who Jesus is, what prayer is, and how Mary fits in all of this. This Gospel calls us to hope despite our doubts, to believe despite our fears, to follow closely even though we misunderstand so much about Jesus or about Mary. Mark is where we see our raw potential as believers. The challenge is to continue to learn, to continue to pray and to continue to persevere despite the pain and the *cost of such discipleship.* Mark's words can help us when we are under the pressure of our own psychic limitations or when we feel rejected or disoriented from what we formerly thought was our security.

Mary emerges in silhouette as the first disciple who breaks down the walls which separate us from Jesus or our fellow-pilgrim disciples. This Gospel represents for us the challenge of *poverty:* simplicity, clear-sightedness; detachment from our securities and culture are called for. Mark's challenge is a "lion's job."

5

Mary in Matthew's Gospel

Discipleship Texts: Matthew 4:18–22; 5:13–16; 8:19; 22; 9:19–13
10:34–41; 16:24–28; 19:23–30

Mary Texts: Matthew 1:1–17; 1:18–25; 2:11, 13–14, 20–21;
12:46–50; 13:53–58

Matthew's image is that of a man. It fits well with the ordered symmetry of his Gospel. For us Matthew is the great architect who has combined the two major liturgical and catechetical documents of his Church: the Gospel of Mark and the Sayings of Jesus to form his Gospel. His literary masterpiece can be described as a pencil-sketch when it comes to those sections where Mary is mentioned. It is the delicate and orderly sketch of an architect; the silhouette of Mark is set aside for the blueprint of Matthew, the man.

What we know of him from a careful study of his work is that his Gospel was written between 89–90 A.D. in an area today known as Syria, and in a city called Antioch where the name "Christian" was first applied to the followers of Jesus: "It was in Antioch that the disciples were called Christians for the first time" (Acts 11:26).

Father Peter Ellis tells us that Matthew could very well have been a converted rabbi. The most recent Catholic commentary written by Father John Meier says, "He was a learned Christian, perhaps a Jew, perhaps a Gentile Semite" (*Matthew—New Testament Message 3*, Wilmington, Delaware: Michael Glazier, 1980, p. xi).

The setting for his writing is a community which is threatened within, that is, a community which easily could be divided against itself. This community, deeply embedded in Jewish origins, had traumatically experienced itself separating from the synagogue "across the street" and had also experienced a great influx of Gentiles into its ranks. "This shift into its Christian existence demanded a new interpretation of old traditions, a new way of looking at Christ and his Church, at the Old Testament and salvation history, at discipleship and morality" (J. Meier, ibid.).

MATTHEW'S SKETCH OF MARY

Matthew's image of Mary can be compared to an artist's delicate sketch. As an author, he is dependent on Mark as a written source. He has an image of Mary from Mark's silhouette; through his own creative talent, he develops it into a sketch which illustrates some unique features in Mary as the Virgin-Mother of Jesus. He has sharpened the silhouette and has presented us with a two-dimensional sketch, so to speak, a pencil-sketch in the first and second chapter of his Gospel. These chapters are called Infancy Narratives.

What are the texts in which Mary appears in Matthew's Gospel?

(1) Mt 1:1–17: an opening genealogy.
(2) Mt 1:18–25: an annunciation to Joseph (a Davidic), with a fulfillment text from Isaiah (Is 7:14).
(3) Mt 2:11, 13–14, 20–21: the child with his Mother.

(4) Mt 12:46–50: the *disciples* are the family of Jesus.

(5) Mt 13:53–58: the rejection of Jesus in his own country.

Matthew's genius can be seen from the composition of chapters 1 and 2. Mark had no hint of such material and traditions. Matthew may have created the content from his own investigation of the traditions about Jesus, the Messiah.

MARY IN THE BIRTH NARRATIVE (CHAPTERS 1—2)

It is within the first two chapters that we find the conception, birth, and infancy of Jesus. These notions are part of Matthew's theology, and they have to be read into our considerations of the later passages in which Mary is mentioned.

One of Matthew's concerns for his Jewish-Christian community is to demonstrate that Jesus fulfilled what was written of him in the Torah-revelation and the prophets. Within these initial chapters, we have five fulfillment texts (Matthew is fond of "fives"—five discourses, five foolish/five wise virgins, the Torah itself, five dreams, etc.).

Perhaps we would do well just to read the five:

(1) *Isaiah 7:14—Mt 1:22–23*
"The maiden is with child and will soon give birth to a son whom she will call Emmanuel."

(2) *Micah 5:1 (2) and 2 Samuel 5:3—Mt 2:5b–6*
"But you, (Bethlehem) Ephrathah, the least of the clans of Judah, out of you will be born for me the one who is to rule over Israel."

(3) *Hosea 11:1—Mt 2:15b*
"I called my son out of Egypt."

(4) *Jeremiah 31:15 (LXX 38:15)—Mt 2:17–18*
"A voice was heard in Ramah, sobbing and loud lamenting; it was Rachel weeping for her children, refusing to be comforted because they were no more."

(5) *Isaiah 4:3 or Judges 16:17—Mt 2:23b*
"He will be called a Nazarene."

These prophecies enable Matthew to affirm that God has prepared for the coming of his Messiah through history. Knowing about Jesus, Matthew rereads these texts as illustrative of who Jesus is and how he fulfilled these prophecies.

Matthew especially wants to present Jesus as the Son of David and as Emmanuel (cf. "God-with-us" or Emmanuel in 1:23; 18:20; 20:28). Who he is and how he is, such are the concerns of Matthew in the opening chapter 1:1–25.

Joseph, not Mary, is the central person in the Annunciation scene of 1:18–25, because Joseph is a Davidid, and as the "legal" father of Jesus he will name the child. Some scholars see Matthew answering the who and how questions in chapter one, while the where and whence are presented in chapter two.

Let us look at the genealogy of 1:1–17.

The inscription is important: "A family record of Jesus Christ, son of David, son of Abraham" (1:1); then the evangelist breaks down the genealogy into three sets of fourteen. Mary does have a significant role in the genealogy—though the descent from David is legally through Joseph. At the very end of the ancestors (1:16) Mary is mentioned: "Mary, of whom was begotten Jesus, who is called the Messiah."

We immediately notice four women are mentioned in the genealogy before Mary: Tamar (Gen 38:24), Rahab (Jos 2:1), Ruth (Ru 3:1–18), and the wife of Uriah, Bathsheba (2 Sam 11). Matthew's intention is to include them; normally Old Testament genealogies rarely mentioned women. The evangelist is trying to tell us something through their being mentioned. There are four theories as to why he mentioned them:

(1) the four women were Gentiles or foreigners;
(2) they were subjects of controversy in the Jewish debate about the Davidic Messiah;
(3) they were sinners (1:23, Jesus is to *save* his people from their sins);
(4) all have irregular marital unions and yet are vehicles of God's messianic plan.

Theory four seems to be the best for helping us understand the role of Mary as Mother of Emmanuel. It is the theory which conforms with the biblical evidence and with the context of Matthew's Gospel. In 1:16 Matthew departs from the "A begot B" pattern of the genealogy. "In each of these prior cases there is a selectivity and a providence exercised by God in the choice of which person propagates the Messianic line" (R. Brown, *et al.*, eds., *Mary in the New Testament*, Philadelphia: Fortress Press/New York: Paulist Press, 1978, p. 82). This theory would highlight verse 16 and the role of Mary within it. Here, too, is an extraordinary marriage resulting in the birth of the Messiah through the prophesied/promised Davidic line.

MATTHEW 1:18–25—JOSEPH AND MARY:
MODELS OF DISCIPLESHIP

This is one of my favorite passages in the Bible. It is described by some scholars as a prolonged footnote to the genealogy of Matthew, but I prefer to see it as a showpiece for the entire Gospel of Matthew; certainly its imaging presents the youthful Mary as Virgin and Mother. This paragraph of Matthew is his sketch of the countenance of Mary. The evangelist also shows us Mary's place in God's plan. The pattern of God's work in salvation history is seen in discontinuity amidst continuity. The virginal conception is the miraculous discontinuity while the legal lineage of David through Joseph is the continuity. Mary's miraculous conception is an eschatological event, and such events are disturbing. Joseph who is "just" is disturbed; the most sensitive conclusion he can reach is to give Mary the document of divorce privately. This would attest to his loyalty and kindness. Often we, too, experience the help of God as Joseph did—through a dream, through our subconscious, or through our memory assisted by the events of Sacred Scripture. Joseph's human calculations and his predicament are solved by God's intervention in a dream.

Just as the great patriarch "Joseph" was a dreamer, so, too, is the foster-father of Jesus. "Joseph, the son of David, is to take Mary into his house, not so much to protect her as to confer Davidic paternity on her child and so insert her child into its proper place in salvation history" (J. Meier, *op. cit.*, p. 7).

To show the continuity of God's love for his people Matthew frequently calls upon the theme of fulfillment of God's promises made known through the Scriptures. Here the text of Isaiah 7:14 is used not in its original Hebrew but from the Greek Septuagint with a few added touches by Matthew himself. The Hebrew text reads: "A young woman shall be with child, and bear a son, and shall name him Emmanuel." Matthew's text reads: "The *virgin* shall be with child and give birth to a son and *they* shall call him Emmanuel." In the context it means what Mary has conceived is of the Holy Spirit; Joseph is to take her as his wife and the child is to be named Jesus (Yahweh helps, Yahweh saves). Matthew uses the Old Testament in such formula quotations or reflection citations twelve times throughout his Gospel. "Each quotation shows that, in Jesus' life, God is carefully ordering history towards the fulfillment of his prophetic word" (J. Meier, *ibid.*, p. 8).

Emmanuel is the name indicated by the text, but Jesus is the name conferred. Both names are important in the Christology of Matthew. The name Jesus or Joshua indicates the salvation of God which will be given to the true Israel, the Church, the community of Matthew; Emmanuel, a name only used in Matthew's Gospel, will show the presence of God among his people. It is used here in Matthew 1:23, then in the ecclesial section 18:20, "Wherever two or three are gathered in my name there am I in their midst." And finally, in the closing section after the apostolic commission; it is the very last phrase of Matthew's Gospel: "And know that I am with you always, until the end of the world" (Mt 28:20).

In verse 24 Matthew returns to his narrative: Joseph, being just, obeys God's command immediately, as he also does in chapter 2. Matthew uses the pattern of command-and-execution of command. This pattern appears a number of times in the Gospel to stress that a true disciple obeys immediately and perfectly. Thus we see Joseph and Mary as models for discipleship.

THE MARRIAGE OF JOSEPH AND MARY

In Galilee the customs surrounding espousals were especially strict. Both the man and woman were to maintain their virginity before actual marriage. At the announcement of their engagement the legal rights of marriage were effective. Should the woman, who usually was no more than twelve years of age, fail in her fidelity during this engagement, it was considered adultery. If her intended spouse took advantage of the conjugal rights with her, this was a serious failing, but not punishable by death. The two already had a contract; the girl usually was living with her relatives during this first stage of betrothal.

The second stage took place usually within a year and consisted in transferral of the young woman to her husband's home. Now he supported her while she had to grind the wheat, cook, wash, take care of the kitchen, nurse her children and by way of compensation weave and sew for him. He had to provide food, clothing, lodging, and burial of her. During the time of Mary and Joseph, the woman's situation was deplorable. She was primarily raised for her fecundity, but was excluded from contact with the worldly domain of men and by no means was she legally considered the equal of her husband.

Mary was pregnant between the two stages of the espousal; hence Joseph's great consternation. He surely was a sensitive man in giving so much thought as to how to handle the dilemma. Normally a direct writ of divorce would have been given, and just as quickly a man would have the woman stoned to death. The situation as described by Matthew in chapter one is softened because of the evangelist's theological intention for writing his Infancy Narrative. Joseph learns in a revelatory dream (one of the usual media for revelation in the Old Testament) that Mary is pregnant by the action of God's power or the Holy Spirit; "the child begotten of her is through (or 'of') the Holy Spirit" (Mt 1:18). Joseph is informed to go through with the second step, the transferral to his home, which would *legally* make Joseph her husband and the legitimate father of the child. The importance of Joseph is, therefore, the reason for Matthew 1:16: "Jacob was the father of Joseph the husband of Mary. It was of her that Jesus who is called the Messiah was born." This legal lineage was as important as the physical begetting of a child; Matthew is careful in giving us the true social and cultural picture of the epoch in which Jesus was born.

The authors of *Mary in the New Testament* clearly bring out the significance of verses 16–25:

> Although Matthew traced Jesus' Davidic ancestry through Joseph, he did not say that Joseph begot the child. The child was begotten through the Holy Spirit; yet he is a true Davidid, for Joseph, "son of David" (1:20), *acknowledged him* by *naming him*. To the angel's message about the conception of the child Matthew adds a formula citation (1:22–23) showing that this conception fulfilled Isaiah's prophecy of a virgin conceiving and bearing a son. He then continues briefly to assure us that Joseph carried out the angel's command—indeed, carried it out so exactly that Mary who had conceived as a virgin remained a virgin till she bore Jesus" (*op. cit.*, p. 85).

In Matthew, Jesus was God's Son from his conception. Mary's conception of Jesus had become a "Christological moment" even as had the baptism and the resurrection. Matthew may have been the first Christian to introduce the theme of a virginal conception, through the Greek version of Isaiah 7:14, using it as a fulfillment citation which is characteristic of his technique. In fact, Matthew often uses a fulfillment text in themes already present in his source (Mark). Would a Christian like Matthew have concluded that since Jesus was God's Son, he had no human father? We must remember that Mark alone calls God Jesus' father.

There are many speculations about the manner in which Matthew reached the idea of a virginal conception:

(1) out of the Isaiah text 7:14;
(2) out of his own belief in it and then using the Isaiah 7:14 text;
(3) as a deduction of his own.

Christian theologians see the text and context of Matthew 1:18–25 as:

(1) a combination of history and theology;
(2) a way of talking about the sinlessness of Jesus;
(3) or even as a pre-Gospel acceptance of such a belief already.

We have noted that Mary (in Matthew's Gospel) has a special place in this birth narrative. Now we are interested in seeing how Matthew has her in chapter two and in the public ministry.

MOTHER AND CHILD (MATTHEW 2)

And going into the house they saw the child with Mary his Mother, and they fell down and worshiped him (2:11).

59

The center of the story of the magi is verse 11—the child and his mother Mary (vv. 11, 13, 14, 20, 21). Joseph is not mentioned in this story; he appears only when needed. Matthew speaks of the child and his Mother four times in this second chapter. The relationship is protected on all fronts by Joseph. Joseph's key role in chapter two is as protector of the family.

> A final word on the historicity of these accounts. Since Matthew and Luke seem to be independent of each other in their infancy narratives, we can be fairly sure that Jesus was born in Bethlehem towards the end of the reign of King Herod, that his mother was Mary and his putative father, Joseph, and that he was brought up in Nazareth. Further, Jesus' Davidic descent and virginal conception are two theological affirmations which clearly existed before Matthew or Luke. But since the two evangelists diverge sharply on other matters, the rest of Matthew's Infancy Narrative may come from scribal use of Old Testament traditions to illumine the full meaning of Christ's birth" (J. Meier, op. cit., p 17).

MARY AND THE ACTIVE MINISTRY OF JESUS

In the active ministry Matthew has no new refernences to Mary beyond those of Mark. Yet, there are significant differences:

> He was still addressing the crowds when his mother and his brothers appeared outside to speak with him. Someone said to him, "Your mother and your brothers are standing out there and they wish to speak to you." He said to the one who had told him, "Who is my mother? Who are my brothers?" Then extending his hand toward his *disciples*, he said, "There are my

mother and my brothers. Whoever does the will of my heavenly Father is brother and sister and mother to me."

For Matthew, the disciples constitute the family of Jesus. Notice how Matthew uses "the disciples" in verse 49 in place of those who are about him. The physical family is seen more as a *catalyst* than a *contrast*. Yet, more important, the *context* is quite different in Matthew, for no longer is Mark's thought present about Jesus' own family thinking that he was beside himself (Mk 3:21); Matthew has omitted this material in his Gospel. Matthew in this section follows Mark's gospel closely but has inserted more of the sayings of Jesus. Matthew, too, presupposes Jesus is in a house. He omits Mark's line that had Jesus' relatives thinking him mad (cf. Mk 3:21). What counts for Matthew is being a disciple in terms of doing the Father's will.

From Matthew 1 and 2 we see that Mary knew of Jesus' special importance through conception, through being saved from a wicked king, through her bringing him to Nazareth. Matthew who has such great reverence for Jesus is also respectful of Mary and the disciples who followed Jesus. He removes most of the misunderstanding and ambiguity which surrounded Mary and the disciples in Mark.

MATTHEW'S FINAL MENTION OF MARY

Jesus next went to his native place and spent his time teaching them in their synagogue. They were filled with amazement, and said to one another, "Where did this man get such wisdom and miraculous powers? Isn't this the carpenter's son? Isn't Mary known to be

61

his mother and James, Joseph, Simon, and Judas his brothers? Aren't his sisters our neighbors? Where did he get all this?" They found him altogether too much for them. Jesus said to them, "No prophet is without honor except in his native place, indeed in his own house." And he did not work many miracles there because of their lack of faith (Mt 13:54–58).

Matthew abbreviates the Markan account: the name of his own country Nazareth is not given, the sabbath is not mentioned, and the disciples are omitted. Jesus who was so carefully listened to is now an object of amazement to his hometown friends. In between the first and the last questions are those which explain why Jesus' wisdom and power do not generate faith at Nazareth. The Nazarenes know him too well. Familiarity breeds contempt, even for the Messiah. There is irony in the way Matthew portrays the people as thinking they know all about Jesus. In reality, their ignorance is abominable. They represent the unbelievers who are scandalized at the flesh of Jesus. "He is not better than the rest of us." Matthew intends them to speak for those who reject Jesus while believing disciples are the true Israel who believe in him.

Matthew also quotes a reference to finding no acceptance among "his relatives" (cf. Mk 6:4); this may be an attempt to soften Mark's hostility toward Jesus' family, though the omission could be explained by Matthew's avoidance of needless repetition. Matthew's reverence for those close to Jesus extends to his relatives as well. They are not among those who do not receive Jesus as a prophet. Matthew also corrects Mark on the statement that "he could do no mighty work there" to "he did not do many mighty works there."

Matthew has already prepared the Christian reader for these difficult lines by means of his Infancy Narrative in chapters one and two. There a positive picture has been presented for these later scenes in which Mary is mentioned. We believers already know of the origins of Jesus Christ, both his divine begetting through the action and power of God's Spirit and through his legitimate human relationship to the family of David because of his legal father, Joseph. Matthew's Gospel is always harmonious with what has been presented from the beginning. Jesus' human family is the foundation for the true Israel which he has formed of all believers through their call to discipleship. Mary and Joseph were the first to respond. Those yet to be baptized can take courage from their example.

SUMMARY OF DISCIPLESHIP IN MATTHEW

Discipleship in Matthew is a call from God that is demanding. Suffering is involved in such a strenuous challenge from God and we, as an entire community, are summoned to obedience and complete dedication to the Father's will. In Matthew's Gospel, discipleship includes the personal revelation given to us in fulfillment of the promises he made to our ancestors in faith, especially Abraham, Sarah, and Moses. The call to discipleship is totally gratuitous and our response should be like that of the first disciples (Peter, Andrew, James and John); it should be immediate and total.

Mary is among those generous disciples in the Gospel of Matthew. In the earliest references to her in the genealogy ("Mary, of whom Jesus was born who is called the Christ"—Mt 1:16) and the short commentary on it (Mt 1:18–25), she is among the "just" persons, like Joseph, who express a life of wholeness dedicated to God. She carries in her person "Emmanuel" (Mt 1:18), the Messiah, who brings salvation to all peoples. Her physical situation of being his mother is transformed into a deeper religious attitude the rest of her life.

The essence of discipleship for Matthew is understanding the call of Jesus. Those who are closely attached to the Son of Man who is also the Son of God really do the will of the Father (Mt 12:46–50) and Mary is among them. This understanding is an opening of one's heart to what God is speaking now and a listening to his revelation.

Faith, too, is essential to discipleship in Matthew's good news. Faith means a willing trust in the fatherly kindness of a God who cares for his people (Mt 6:30), who hears their prayers (Mt 17:20; 21:20–22) and who supports them with his power (Mt 8:10, 13; 9:2, 22, 28f; 18:28). Mary has such faith as the Mother of the Messiah. She holds firmly to the covenant, to God's promise and to the Mosaic law. This holding firm in faith (the Hebrew word "Amen" comes from the word used for a faith that is solid) is Mary's trust and obedience.

To be a disciple of Jesus means to be one of the little ones (*mikroi*): "I assure you, unless you change and become like little children you will not enter the kingdom of God. Whoever makes himself lowly, becoming like this child, is of greatest importance in the heavenly reign" (Mt 18:3–4). This saying of Jesus is related to what is found in the first four beatitudes which speak of the essence of discipleship:

> How blest are the poor in spirit; the reign of God is theirs.
> Blest too are the sorrowing; they shall be consoled.
> Blest are the lowly; they shall inherit the land.
> Blest are they who hunger and thirst for holiness; they shall have their fill (Mt 5:3–6).

For Matthew the beatitudes introduce the great charter—
the Sermon on the Mount—of discipleship (chapters 5—
7). Mary is called blessed or happy in the Gospel of Luke
(1:42, 45; 11:27–28). Here, in Matthew, the first four beatitudes are her Magnificat in action. Through them she
has the Gospel within her, enabling her to live out the
good news so perfectly. Hers is the full response of a
woman who has been surprised by the joy of God's love.
She, like Jesus, is a happy person—a beatitude in action.

For Matthew, the heavenly Father is transcendent
and holy—"Be ye perfect as your heavenly Father is perfect" (Mt 5:48). Therefore, our call demands a conversion,
that is, a *metanoia*, a change of heart, a topsy-turvy of our
self-protective values. Mary, the perfect disciple, fulfilled
her call as the Virgin-Mother who brought forth her Son
(Emmanuel) who is God-with-us (Mt 1:23; see also 18:20;
28:20). She does the will of the Father just as Jesus and
Joseph do the will of the heavenly Father.

Finally, through Matthew we come to appreciate the
call to discipleship as a call to be shared with others in the
Christian community. Matthew summons us to teach all
ethnics and to baptize them into the good news of Jesus
Christ:

> Go, therefore, and make disciples of all the nations.
> Baptize them in the name of the Father and of the Son
> and of the Holy Spirit (Mt 28:19).

It is in this Gospel that we find the call especially difficult, for Jesus even says, "Follow me, and leave the dead
to bury their dead" (8:22). Father William Thompson, S.J.
summarizes the challenge: "When a disciple experiences
a conflict of loyalties to Jesus or to his own family, he

must choose to follow Jesus (*The Bible Today*, 19, January 1981, p. 18). And he further asserts (p. 24):

> The pattern of experience of the disciples in Matthew bears strong resemblance to our own experience. To follow Jesus means to move between enthusiasm and fear, faith and doubt, understanding and misunderstanding, suffering and hope, failure and mission. Basic to the Christian life in any age, the tension created by such movement will enable us to witness to the Kingdom in our time, as they did in theirs.

6

Mary in Luke's Gospel

Discipleship Texts: Luke 1:26–38; 2:19, 51; 11:1/Acts 1:14

Mary Texts: Luke, chapters 1 and 2 (especially: 1:26–38; 1:39–56; 2:1–20; 2:21–40); 3:23; 4:16–30; 8:19–21; 11:27–28/Acts 1:14

LUKE'S PORTRAIT OF MARY

By far, Luke's portrait of Mary as the perfect disciple is the most complete and ecclesial one. The image of Luke's portrait is that of an oil painting. History attests to the choice, for more than any other Gospel, Luke's has been chosen by the greatest artists for subject matter and scenes. Could it be that the legend of Luke first painting a portrait of Mary stems from the inspiration that he has given to true artists after him? Yes, in a real sense, Luke, through his literary presentations, paints colorful scenes of Mary and Jesus in his Infancy Narrative. It is his oil painting which reveals Mary's personality more than other forms of art.

The Gospel of Luke and his second work, Acts, contain more texts, both quantitatively and qualitatively, which mention Mary than the rest of the New Testament. In the Infancy Narratives the earliest reflection about

Mary is offered by Luke in the Annunciation Narrative (Lk 1:26–38).

SOURCES

Luke's Gospel is more literary and developed than that of Mark, though we know that Luke used Mark's material (over one-third of his texts). The sources of Luke were Mark's Gospel, the Sayings of Jesus (Q) and special material that only Luke has recourse to, plus much material that he himself created. His Gospel comes in the third generation after the death of Jesus—around 85 A.D. It is at this epoch that questions arose within the Christian communities about the origins of Jesus. Where was he born? Of whom? Why was he born of Mary of Nazareth? What do we know of his mother and his relatives? Luke pondered over these questions more than did the other evangelists:

> Many have undertaken to compile a narrative of events which have been fulfilled in our midst, precisely as those events were transmitted to us by the original eyewitnesses and ministers of the word. I too have carefully traced the whole sequence of events from the beginning, and have decided to set it in writing for you, Theophilus, so that Your Excellency may see how reliable the instruction was that you received (Lk 1:1–4).

From the sparse information in Mark we can assume that the first Gospel writer had no interest in these questions about Jesus' origins. It is Luke who makes up for the lack of evidence in Mark; we are moving from a silhouette of Mary to a sweeping canvas painting of the Virgin Mother.

Luke was not an eyewitness to the events of Jesus. He

68

may never have become familiar with the territory of Jesus—Israel. And he may never have met or known Mary of Nazareth, the Mother of Jesus. Though older scholars have suggested that Luke composed his Infancy Narrative after conferring with Mary, the mother of Jesus, there is no evidence in the texts themselves that this is the case. Luke as a man faithful to the tradition about Jesus did comb the fields of tradition for finding as much information as he could about Mary, but this oral tradition about the birth and early years of Jesus never was put into writing prior to Luke. Hence his narrative is crucial for our image of Mary in the twentieth century. If he had not written about Mary, would we have developed such an interest and devotion to Mary? I think not. Mariology would have been an impossibility, because of the impoverished sources.

What are the scenes he paints? In chapters one and two of his Gospel, Luke gives us the texts pertaining to the response of Mary, to her conceiving and to the birth and youth of Jesus. Only in Luke do we have the process of "before," "during," and "after" the birth inferred. Undoubtedly, theologians of the fifth and sixth centuries, that is, the Fathers of the Church, took their notion of Mary as Virgin Mother from the Gospel of Luke. It is from them that we have the notion of her *perpetual* (a non-New Testament word) virginity, before, during, and after the birth of Jesus.

A GLANCE AT THE WHOLE CANVAS: THE SEQUENCE OF MARIAN TEXTS

Luke does give prominence to Mary more than the other evangelists. She is at the center of several scenes within his first two chapters, not as a symbolic image, but as a real historical person, Mary of Nazareth, the Mother of Jesus. In Luke 1:26–38 the announcement of the birth of Jesus is made to Mary, not to Joseph as we saw in the more Jewish Gospel of Matthew. Mary parallels—like a diptych—the annunciation made to Zechariah in Jerusalem at the temple about John the Baptist (cf. Lk 1:8–25 and 1:26–38). The Annunciation can be seen as the calling of Mary to discipleship.

Mary visits her cousin Elizabeth (Lk 1:39–45), the mother of John the Baptist, and it is Elizabeth who first greets her in the most ancient of prayers dedicated to Mary, the Hail Mary—Elizabeth together with what Gabriel has announced is our source for this prayer. In Luke 1:43 Mary is greeted as "the mother of the Lord.".

In Mary's reciting her hymn of praise, the Magnificat (Lk 1:46–55), we have an example of biblical prayer which can and is used in our liturgies, particularly Evensong.

She also gives birth to Jesus at Bethlehem (Lk 2:1–20).

After the circumcision of her child, she presents Jesus in the temple and is greeted by Simeon (Lk 2:21–40).

She features prominently in the finding of the child Jesus in the temple (Lk 2:41–52).

These events in which Mary has such a large part will be easily recognized as the set of joyful mysteries of the rosary which give this particular prayer a biblical foundation based on divine revelation in the Scriptures.

One begins to notice what a fine literary artist Luke is. He even imitates the ancient language of the Septuagint to recapture the flavor of an ancient setting in introducing the entire Infancy Narrative (1:5–2:52).

In 8:19–21 Luke recounts the incident of the Mother (Mary) and the brothers. Luke is dependent on Mark for these verses.

In 11:27–28 the woman from the crowd praises Mary.

This is another blessedness-saying or a beatitude about Mary.

In Acts 1:14 we see Mary in Jerusalem praying with the assembled *believers*. She as a believing disciple is the only bridge from the birth of Christ to the birth of the Church in Luke just as she was the bridge for the hidden years of Jesus and his active ministry.

The third evangelist is the evangelist of the Holy Spirit and of the poor (*anawim*); he is the one who for the first time in the history of the Christian community entered into reflections of a personal nature about Mary. It would take until the fourth century for the Fathers of the Church to so enter into the mind and heart of Mary again.

Luke preached the Gospel in a universal way so that the history of salvation would reach the hearts of all men and women. With Paul he has written almost fifty percent of the New Testament. Some even attribute parts of John's Gospel (for example, Jn 8:1–11; Jn 21) and the Letter to the Hebrews to Luke. Undoubtedly he painted the most pictures with words about Jesus and his friends— therefore he was in the tradition called an artist. His careful treatment of sickness and his ability to describe the diseases and cures has also enabled Paul to speak of him as "Luke, dear and beloved physician" (Col 4:14).

Another characteristic that he shares with us is that he is a sensitive and caring person who has modeled his life on the kindness and compassionate love of God. It is he who tells us; "Be ye compassionate even as your heavenly Father is compassionate" (Lk 6:36), while Matthew has said, "Be ye perfect even as the Father is perfect" (Mt 5:48).

With these characteristics of Luke in mind we can better appreciate the presence of Mary of Nazareth in his Infancy Narrative. The first scene, the Annunciation, is characteristically Lucan: joy, the presence of the Spirit and salvation. We shall now look sequentially at the individual tableaus of the Lucan canvas.

A STUDY OF THE PAINTINGS

1. *Mary's Call to Discipleship*—The Annunciation (Lk 1:26–38)

Mary conceives Jesus. Here is the most Marian scene of all that we will see. More literature, art, and poetry have centered on this than any other passage in the New Testament. (And yet we must remember that Jesus is still the primary emphasis for Luke.) Luke in using the literary-form of the Annunciation has a host of similar annunciations to draw from in the Old Testament: to Abraham (Gen 17), to Samson's parents (Jgs 13), to Moses (Ex 3), to Gideon (Jgs 6). We have also seen that Matthew uses an annunciation to Joseph (Mt 1:20–23). Luke also has an annunciation to Zechariah and to the shepherds (Lk 1:8–23; 2:8–20).

2. *Mary Visits Elizabeth* (Lk 1:39–45)

The message of good news is to be shared. This is basically the reason Mary visits Elizabeth. Everyone in the initial scenes of this Gospel is set in movement by the Spirit, for the central event of all salvation is taking place. We can see ourselves in the hastening of Mary to Elizabeth as religious persons who fulfill our mission, our apostolate. The Dominicans have an expression, "to contemplate and then to share this contemplation with others." Mary continues to be the obedient handmaid of the Lord. Luke shows this by saying that Mary went *with haste* to the house of Zechariah—some seventy to ninety miles of travel by foot.

2.1 *Elizabeth's Hymn to Mary* (Lk 1:42–45)

Elizabeth was filled with the Holy Spirit and cried out in a loud voice: "Blest are you among women and blest is the fruit of your womb. But who am I that the mother of my Lord should come to me? The moment your greeting sounded in my ears, the baby leapt in my womb for joy. Blest is she who trusted that the Lord's words to her would be fulfilled."

Some see in Elizabeth's words the first hymn to Mary. Elizabeth extols in hymnic form the greatness of Mary: "The mother of my Lord." Elizabeth, too, is filled with the Holy Spirit and her baby leaps within her womb. Mary's cousin praises her in the same fashion that Deborah praised Jael—"Blessed be Jael among women" (Jgs 5:24). The blessing she pronounces is also a form of beatitude in the sense that Elizabeth recognizes already that Mary is in a state of joy and happiness because God has favored her. Both *blessed* and *beatitude* are used in Luke's text (*eulogomene*, v. 42 and *makaria*, v. 45). Mary has been recognized as a woman of faith and as a disciple who is obedient to God's word, that is, to the actual salvific events accomplished by God among his people (cf. Dt 28:1, 4). In Mary's own prior response to Gabriel she shows the spontaneous reaction of a woman totally dependent on God: "I am the Lord's handmaid. Let it be with me as you say" (Lk 1:38).

The beatitude of v. 45 will be again expressed by a woman who declares that Jesus' mother is truly a fortunate person (cf. Lk 11:27–28). Both sayings compliment the mother of Jesus—the first directly and explicitly, the second implicitly because of who Jesus is. Father Fitzmyer succinctly tells us the meaning of this passage:

In the visitation scene proper Mary's child is there recognized as the Kyrios (Lord), and Mary as the "mother of the Lord," a believer, a model of faith. Luke is picking up the lowly handmaid motif of 1:38 and making her a disciple from the beginning of his accounts (cf. 8:19–21; Acts 1:14) (J. Fitzmyer, *Luke, The Anchor Bible—Volume 28*, New York: Doubleday & Co., 1981, p. 358).

3. *The Song of Mary, Her Magnificat* (Lk 1:46–55)

Mary responds to Elizabeth's hymn of praise by her own song, her Magnificat, which reverberates with echoes of the Psalms, of Hannah's praise of God (1 Sam 2:1–10) and of other parts of the Hebrew Scriptures. Mary as a Jewish woman sings in the manner of her people praising God for his mercy and love toward her and for his strong fidelity to the convenants made with her ancestors—Abraham and the patriarchs. Mary is self-confident and free because she centers on the power and presence of God in her own soul and memory of her people, Israel. Her song is a fitting and necessary conclusion to her meeting with Elizabeth. She calls herself the handmaid (*doule* in Greek means "slave-girl") of the Lord. We have seen how Jesus, too, is the servant or slave of God (cf. Phil 2:7). Mary "exults in God her Savior" (Hb 3:18). Her "Lord has looked upon his lowly handmaid (1 Sam 2:1). God's "name is holy" and "his mercy reaches from age to age for those who fear him" (Pss 111:9; 103:17). "He has pulled down princes and exalted the lowly" (Jb 5:11; 12:19). She prays: "The hungry he has filled with good tidings" (Ps 107:9) and "He has come to the help of Israel his servant, mindful of his mercy" (Ps 98:3; Is 41:8–9).

4. *Mary and the Birth at Bethlehem* (Lk 2:1–20)

Throughout chapter two, Mary has a significant role which begins with the birth of Jesus. This is our primary source for celebrating the beautiful feast of Christmas (Lk 2:1–20). The census of Augustus is used by Luke as a way of leading the reader to a new understanding of the universalism of Christianity as part of the Roman Empire. It is no underground movement. Christianity is a licit religion (*religio licita*) which respects the human authority of the Roman Empire. Luke will elaborate on this more significantly in his second volume, Acts, in which the growth and development of Christianity are presented for the first time in an orderly yet idyllic manner.

Joseph, the husband of Mary, now emerges in Luke's narrative as an equal partner to Mary. He, too, is significant, for Luke is indicating the Davidic origins of the child to be born by writing that, because of the census of Augustus, Joseph goes with Mary from Nazareth to David's town of Bethlehem in Judea. He is clearly descended from the house and family of David (Lk 2:4). Mary, once again, is called the betrothed or fiancée of Joseph. Luke has prepared the reader with a compact preface for the birth of Jesus. Verses 6–7 give us the simplicity and common condition of Jesus' birth:

> And while they were there the time came for her to be delivered. And she gave birth to her first-born son and wrapped him in cloth bands, and laid him in a manger, because there was no place for them in the lodge.

Luke, as we have seen above, parallels the birth of the Baptist with the birth of Jesus (Lk 1:57–58; 2:6–7), just as he had paired the annunciation to Zechariah with that made to Mary. He will continue the use of such diptychs in the circumcision and naming of John and Jesus (Lk 1:59–63; 2:21). Throughout the rest of the Infancy Narrative, Luke will make use of Old Testament motifs; for example, for the cloth bands which surround the body, Wisdom 7:4–5: "In swaddling clothes and with constant care I was nurtured. For no king has any different origin or birth"; for the manger, Isaiah 1:3: "An ox knows its owner and an ass the manger of its lord; but Israel knows not me, and my people does not comprehend." Luke is aware of Micah 5:1f for understanding the fulfillment of the Davidic claims of the Messiah at Bethlehem. The birth of the Messiah in such humble surroundings enables the believer to understand that Jesus will not be a political or warrior-like Messiah.

4.1 *The Shepherds* (Lk 2:8–20)

Luke surrounds the rest of the birth narrative by means of the announcement to the shepherds (vv. 8–14) and the discovery of the child with Mary and Joseph by these simple people who depend on God. The theme of the poor and the sick so prevalent in the rest of Luke is being foreshadowed in these pericopes. The shepherds fit in with Luke's telling us that Jesus is born in Bethlehem (the house of bread), and, more important, Bethlehem is the location where the shepherd David is first anointed king (1 Sam 16:4, 18). We should recall Luke 1:38–52 where the evangelist emphasizes God's predilection for the lowly of human society.

In the announcement of the event of Jesus' birth the shepherds are told of a Savior who is the Anointed One (Christ) and the Lord! It would take until the actual historical development of the early Christian communities to comprehend the meaning of those titles applied to Jesus. Here we have more the faith of Luke than that of the shepherds in using such names for Jesus. Father Fitzmyer in his excellent Anchor Bible commentary brings this out as well:

> The three christological titles applied to Jesus in this scene are titles born of resurrection-faith, which are being pressed back to the very beginning of his earthly existence" (*op. cit.*, p. 397).

The hymn of the angels or "Glory to God in the highest" continues the joyous praise of God that we find in the Magnificat of Mary and the Benedictus of Zechariah.

Luke skillfully describes the visit of the shepherds and their joyful reaction which results in praise of God. He deftly concludes the birth with Mary's keeping all these things or events while pondering them over in her heart (Lk 2:19). She as the first Christian believer attempts to plumb the meaning of God's action among his people through the birth of her Son, but she, too, as a believer cannot comprehend the full significance of the happening. Luke returns to the same refrain when we see Mary finding Jesus in the temple as the Infancy Narrative comes to a close (Lk 2:51). She will also be present as a prayerful person among the disciples when Jesus continues in his Church at Pentecost (Acts 1:14). Luke may not only be hinting that Mary is an image of the Church, but in his portrayal of her he may be indicating what it means to be a member of the Church. Mary's attitude as a believing woman and as a disciple is seen in 1:38–45 and her inner reflection in 2:19, 51. Her humility, acceptance, and obedience to the word of God makes of her a believer-disciple for "those who, hearing the word, hold it fast in an honest and good heart and bring forth fruit with patience" (Lk 8:15). Complete discipleship is not possible until the work of God has been proclaimed in its fullness, not only during the public ministry of Jesus, but also on the cross and through the resurrection. Mary will experience the call of discipleship in every stage of her Son's life and even in the life of his Church.

5. *Naming of Jesus and Purification of Mary* (Lk 2:21–40)

Luke continues to parallel the events of John the Baptist with Mary's Son, Jesus. In the final part of the Infancy Narrative (Lk 2:21–40) the naming of Jesus is given at the time of his circumcision, and forty days after his birth he is made manifest through the prophetic proclamation of Simeon and the saintly prophetic presence of Anna. Luke always balances the mention of man with that of woman. This stems from his sensitivity to all persons and from his universalism. This section of the narrative is also presented against the background of traditional Jewish piety. Mary and Joseph are among the *anawim* (the poor ones who totally depend on God) and who fulfill the righteousness and holiness of God's revelation to his people. Simeon and Anna belong to the *anawim* in their faithful expectation of the visiting presence of the Lord and his salvation. Jesus, the newborn child, is that salvation presented to Israel and to the Gentiles. Joseph and Mary fulfill the prescriptions of the rite of purification and Mary becomes involved in the future mission of her child through the prophetic manifestation of Simeon.

Simeon's canticle has to be understood as a revelation both to Israel and to all peoples. Mary is to be caught in the agony of decision which centers in the mission of her Son. She, too, will grow in her faith-relationship to God's will through her Son and the discriminating sword will pierce her heart. Father Fitzmyer has summarized Mary's role in these scenes:

Mary too will be caught in this critical aspect of his mission. For the discriminating sword will pierce her soul too. She will learn what division can come into a family by the role that her son is to play, for her relation to him will be not merely maternal but one transcending such familial ties, viz., that of the faithful disciple. Simeon's words to Mary about the sword foreshadow, in effect, Jesus' answer to the woman who uttered a beatitude over Mary for having given birth to such a son; he replied, "Blessed rather are those who hear the word of God and observe it" (Lk 11:28; cf. 8:21) (*ibid.*, p. 423).

6. *Mary and the Finding of Jesus in the Temple Area* (Lk 2:41–52)

Luke could have logically ended the Infancy Narrative with 2:40 where he summarizes the first stages of Jesus' growth as a child who grew and was strengthened in wisdom with the favor of God upon him, just as Mary at the Annunciation was considered to be the "favored one of God" (1:28).

Once again, however, we are brought back to the holy city of Jerusalem in the last scene of the Holy Family as its years of privacy are brought to a close by Luke. The atmosphere of piety and reverence felt in the Presentation scene continues here in the temple area twelve years later as Mary, Joseph and Jesus are in Jerusalem for the celebration of the Passover festival. Jesus remains in Jerusalem on his own. This leads to a confrontation with Mary and Joseph when they do find him and Luke presents us with the first words of Jesus: "Why are you searching for me? Did you not know that I must be about the concerns of my Father?" (Lk 2:49). Since Luke has surrounded the scene with the notion of the wisdom of Jesus, we should not be surprised to find that these first words of Jesus bear upon his relationship to God as his Father. What is surprising is the reaction of his parents (especially in the light of Lk 1:32–35; 2:11, 17, 19).

Luke, undoubtedly, was concerned about how to conclude the early life of Jesus. The scene is not described accurately as belonging to the Infancy Narrative (Lk 1:5–2:40); rather it shows us Jesus coming into adulthood. Luke uses the episode as a transition to what is to follow in the rest of the Gospel. Through his skillful literary touch, Luke ties this scene to what has preceded (see 2:51–52; cf. 2:19). He also highlights a theme he is particularly fond of—Jerusalem and the temple (Lk 1:5–25; 2:22–38; 24:53).

The basic story-line of the finding in the temple is similar to Jesus' first confrontation with his mother and relatives in Mark 3:20–35. There is a search on their part for Jesus; they find him inside a house speaking about the relationship he wishes all to have with his heavenly Father. His mother and brothers seem to have difficulty in understanding him. In fact, his relatives may have thought him to be "beside himself" or "insane" (Mk 3:21; *exeste*). In verse 47 of the Lucan narrative the same verb is used of those hearing him—they were amazed or beside themselves (*existanto*). Only afterward do they come to comprehend the deeper intentions of Jesus when he speaks of his relationship to his Father. There is a return to his native Nazareth in both Mark and Luke, and then the active ministry of Jesus begins anew in Mark and for the first time in Luke.

Mary is the active protagonist in this temple scene and will have the same role in Jesus' first sign in John's Gospel at the wedding feast of Cana which also happens "on the third day." Luke tells us that Mary and Joseph are startled when they find Jesus (Lk 2:48). Mary's confrontation effort is met with the mysterious response of Jesus, "Did you not know I had to be about my Father's concerns?" This divine necessity of accomplishing the will of the Father is thematic to Luke (9:22; 13:33; 17:25; 22:37). Jesus' response is not gruff, but the distancing of Jesus from his earthly parents in favor of his relationship to his Father has begun. Mary thus experienced Simeon's oracle about the sword, and Luke is giving evidence of how the sword of discrimination spoken of by Simeon pierces Mary's soul. She has to grow again and again into understanding the events and sayings of her Son. Her lack of comprehension shows the need for her to grow in faith. She ponders over once again the events that have happened and, now, the scene in the temple area confirms the necessity to grow further in understanding her Son's relationship to God his Father and her own relationship to that same God. Only when his passion, death, and resurrection are completed will the fullness of discipleship be realized in Mary. But in the meantime, Mary is present at this scene as a woman of faith and, like ourselves, must grow in that faith. The sword of discrimination pierces her heart at each of these manifestations of her Son, but through her deepening and unswerving faith and trust, these events and sayings which she pondered in her heart result in her becoming a woman of faith for all times.

7. *Mary in the Public Ministry* (Lk 8:19–21; 11:27–28)

After chapters one and two Mary is not mentioned specifically by name. There are several references to the Mother of Jesus in 8:19–21 and 11:27–28 which are not different from what Mark and Matthew had said. She is mentioned as being present in Jesus' ministry on these occasions to show continuity with the traditions that Luke was aware existed in Mark.

His mother and his brothers came to him, but they were unable to get near him because of the crowd. It was reported to him, "Your mother and your brothers are standing outside wishing to see you." He, however, answered them, "My mother and my brothers are those who hear the word of God and act on it" (Lk 8:19–21).

In comparison with Mark and Matthew, Luke has taken this story and transposed it as well as placed it in a positive context. This saying of Jesus affirms that his mother and his brothers are faithful disciples who hear the word of God and act on it. We must remember the importance of action in the Jewish authors. Just as God's word is always effective, so, too, must the disciple do more than hear it. Luke has removed any negative connotations that he may have seen in Mark's account in 3:31–35. There is no question of Jesus pointing toward those seated around him. There is no dramatic contrast in Luke. He simply says, "My mother and my brothers are the ones who listen to the word of God and act upon it." Luke uses present participles to describe this action, that is, they continue to hear God's word and they are always accomplishing it. This in biblical language is the equivalent of doing the will of God. This is what a disciple of Jesus is called to do.

This incident is also carefully placed within a section of Luke's Gospel that treats of the word of God through the parable of the sower and of the saying of Jesus about the light not to be hidden under a cover. Thus Jesus' mother and brothers are those who listen with a noble and generous mind (cf. Lk 8:15). Father Fitzmyer comments:

Jesus' reply does not imply a denial of family ties or a criticism of his kin; it does imply that another relationship to himself can transcend even that of family ties. Genuine relation to him consists not so much in descent from common ancestry as a voluntary attachment involving the acceptance of God's word, which he preaches, as the norm of one's life. Here Jesus' mother and brothers are shown to be prime examples of that relation (*ibid.*, p. 723).

The last mention of Jesus' mother in Luke's Gospel is the following:

It happened that while he was saying these things a woman in the crowd raised her voice and said to him, "Blessed is the womb which carried you and the breasts which nursed you." He, however, replied, "Blessed rather are those who are hearing the word of God and keeping it" (Lk 11:27–28).

The exclamation centered upon Jesus, a person who made a great impression upon this unknown woman. Her shout may have been extravagant. Jesus uses the occasion to contrast who he is with what he has been called to, namely, the hearing and accomplishing of the will of God. Indirectly, the beatitude is thus applied to those who do the same. Mary, the Mother of Jesus, would be among the blessed. Jesus again is suggesting that obedient retention of God's word is the most important thing. The ecumenical effort on a study of this passage in *Mary in the New Testament* has this conclusion:

In the overall Lucan picture of Mary, 11:28 stresses that Jesus' mother is worthy of a beatitude, yet not simply because she has given birth to a child. Her beatitude must be based on the fact that she had heard, believed, obeyed, kept and pondered the word, and continued to do it (Acts 1:14). Implicitly, 11:28 is a more positive way of expressing that, like all others, Mary too must meet the criterion of discipleship. She herself predicted: "Behold, henceforth all generations will call me happy" (1:48), but now we have come to understand why (*op. cit.*, p. 172).

Luke's final touch-up of the portrait of Mary makes her a fortunate, a happy, a smiling woman. This woman has received her title of blessed or happy virgin from Luke's Gospel.

8. *Mary, an Image of the Church* (Acts 1:14)

These all were devoting themselves with one accord to prayer, together with women, and Mary, the mother of Jesus, and together with his brothers.

The reference to Mary in Acts 1:14 is the last mention of her in the New Testament. By her presence in the upper room, Mary becomes the only "disciple" of Jesus who has bridged every stage of his life from conception to birth, infancy, adolescence, active ministry and now to his new birth in the primitive community or the nascent Church. All of those present, both men and women, are one in Jesus (cf. Gal 1:28). Mary is the only woman singled out by name. Luke may be paralleling the beginning of his second work with that of his Gospel. The conception and birth of Jesus parallels the birth of the Church.

There is a deliberateness about Luke's mention of Mary here. It may be more a theological and literary intention than his focusing on something historical. If theological in intent, it has a certain similarity to the presence of Mary at the foot of the cross in John's Gospel (Jn 19:25–27). The image of the Church is emerging within this summary statement of Luke. Mary is within and among this community of believing disciples and is, so to speak, the first among equals. She is part of the praying community represented here. The words Luke uses stress the unanimity of the community (*homothumadon*). This term is used for the actions which constitute the community of the risen Lord through prayer (Acts 1:14; 2:1, 46; 4:24; 5:12) and very soon through apostolic teaching (Acts 8:6; 20:18). This community unanimity is a gift of God for the praise of God. Mary, who is central to this event, is the praying disciple. She has met the criterion of the perfect disciple of Jesus from the Annunciation (1:26–35) and during the ministry (8:19–21). She, with the other disciples, demonstrates the continuity between the historical Jesus and the believing community—the risen body of Christ—which is the Church.

In summarizing the importance of Mary for Luke, the ecumenical task force in *Mary in the New Testament* says:

> He (Luke) is content in his last mention of Mary to show her of one accord with those who would constitute the nascent Church at Pentecost, engaged in prayer that would so mark the life of that Church (Acts 2:42; 6:4; 12:5). He may not have known much about her subsequent life, but he has taken care to give a consistent picture of her from the first Annunication of the good news to the eve of the coming of the spirit who would empower the spread of that good news from Jerusalem to the end of the earth (Acts 1:8). Mary's first response to the good news was: "Behold the handmaid of the Lord. Let it be to me according to your word." The real import of Acts 1:14 is to remind the reader that she had not changed her mind (*ibid.*, p. 177).

MARY AS THE DISCIPLE OF PRAYER IN LUKE-ACTS

One of the characteristics of a disciple is that the person be close to Jesus and follow him. This closeness is brought about especially through a prayerful attitude and union with the Lord. We see this in Luke's Gospel:

> One day he was praying in a certain place. When he had finished, one of his *disciples* asked him, "Lord, teach us to pray, as John taught his disciples" (Lk 11:1).

We know the prayer Jesus taught them: the Lord's Prayer. Perhaps what we do not remember is that Luke is the evangelist who emphasizes that prayer is at the heart of the discipleship to which we are called. If the renunciations demanded by this discipleship are to be understood and accepted, we must have the ability to pray and not to lose heart; we must have the courage to persevere.

The Lucan image of Mary is of a perfect disciple precisely because she prays. She is a witness to prayer within the Gospel just as Jesus himself is. In fact there are nineteen occasions in the twenty-four chapters of Luke where prayer is thematic. Let us turn to those in which Mary is involved. Mary, the Mother of Jesus, is a person of profound prayer. In the Annunciation in Luke (1:26–38), she is presented as a young woman open to the plan of God. As a devout Jewess, she follows the will of God through her Jewish heritage of the Torah and through her belonging to a covenanted people of God, called Israel. God had spoken to her ancestors through Moses who received the revelation of God on Mount Sinai in the gift of the Torah. In turn, each succeeding Jew of all generations firmly believed that the will of God is found in the Torah. Mary, too, was born again on Mount Sinai through this Mosaic revelation. It is within such a perspective and background that the Gospel writer St. Luke speaks to us about her, about who she is, how she prays, and how God loves her in a special way.

Luke presents Mary as a woman and disciple of prayer in three ways.

First, Mary is a person who *articulates* the promises of God made to his people. Her articulation flows from the inspired words of the Hebrew Scriptures which form the core of her hymn praising God (the Magnificat: Lk 1:46–55).

Second, Mary prays through her profound *reflection on the events* in which she is involved in the mystery of *salvation history* (the Annunciation, the birth of Jesus, the presentation in the temple, and the finding in the temple). Luke uses this phrase to express this second mode of her prayer. "But Mary kept with concern all events interpreting them in her heart" (Lk 2:19). And some dozen years later, at the end of the scene in which Jesus is found in the temple, she again is presented by the evangelist as praying in this reflective way: "His mother kept with concern all these events in her heart" (Lk 2:51).

Finally, a third mode of her prayer—*prayer within and for a community*—is found in Acts 1:14. "All these joined in continuous prayer, together with several women, including Mary the mother of Jesus, and his brothers."

When reading or praying biblical texts, it is helpful to understand the mode, the atmosphere, and the overall context through which the sacred writer conveys his inspired message. The two texts of Luke 2:19, 51 are within the context of the entire Infancy Narrative. Mary is among those inspired by the Holy Spirit in the salvific events narrated in a special way by St. Luke. In addition, among all those mentioned: Zechariah, Elizabeth, Simeon and Anna, she (Mary) is special, for Luke employs these two phrases only for her and not for the others. Mary alone is the bridge between the Infancy Narrative and the ministry of Jesus. She alone is present from the birth of Jesus to the birth of the Church (Acts 1:14). This means that, based on the fact of Jesus' birth, there are no believing disciples except Mary. Mary is a model for our faith, for she is the most experienced of disciples, knowing him from the crib to the cross; and again when the fullness of Jesus' Spirit comes at Pentecost, she is present as a disciple among other disciples.

These two phrases (Lk 2:19, 51) describing Mary's concern about the sacred events which surround Jesus, her Son, as an infant and as a young boy approaching manhood are important signposts. These verses enable us to look at an aspect of her interior disposition—her prayer life, if you will. This form of biblical reflection is suggested as a help for our own prayer life in the modern atmosphere in which we live. Perhaps this form of prayer is necessary for spiritual growth if we are to advance in age, wisdom and grace. We grow from prayer through prayer.

From the inarticulate sounds and groans of our body we yearn to be free through the Spirit. We, too, groan inwardly as we await for our bodies to be set free. The Spirit, too, comes to help us in our weakness. For when we cannot choose words in order to pray properly, the Spirit himself expresses our plea in a way that could never be put into words, and God who knows everything in our hearts knows perfectly well what he means, and that the pleas of the saints expressed by the Spirit are according to the mind of God (Rom 8:23–27).

There is no explicit example of Mary praying in this inarticulate fashion, but she does pray in an articulate manner in her Magnificat. In this prayer she praises her Lord while remembering his promises to Abraham and his people. This is a form of prayer in which we participate when we pray the Psalms or make up our own hymns and psalms which praise and thank the Lord.

The pondering over in her heart is a third form of biblical prayer. Scholars have seen this form in the context of the Wisdom books of the Scripture. Thus Mary is presented to us as the wise virgin or as a model of a woman of wisdom. The first evident parallel to the Lucan phrases 2:19, 51 is found in the mature and sagacious Jacob "who keeps the event of the dream of his son Joseph in mind" (Gen 37:11). (The same expression is used in the Septuagint Greek as that of Luke 2:19, 51.)

In Daniel 7:28, at the end of his vision of the four beasts it is said: "I kept the word in my heart." The text looks toward the future in both Daniel and Genesis. Mary, in the context of the shepherd scene of chapter two of Luke, is also depicted as the one most concerned by the vision of the shepherds, for she "kept all these words (or events) in her heart" (Lk 2:19). Luke has revealed what Mary is pondering over with great concern. In verse eleven the object of that pondering is mentioned: "For today is born for you a Savior who is Christ the Lord in the city of David." To understand correctly the meaning of Lk 2:19, 51 the entire section on the shepherds and the conclusion to the Infancy Narrative have to be seen within the structural design and context of the whole Infancy Narrative. This fact has already been stressed in showing how Mary is the only person in these scenes to act as a bridge from his birth to the active ministry of Jesus. The juxtaposition of verses 18 and 19 sets Mary apart from all others in her wonder (and prayer) at the mystery of her child.

In the overall context of the Infancy Narrative and for the whole work of Luke/Acts, the Holy Spirit or the power of God moves within the hearts of people. And whenever the Spirit is presented, concrete, real, wondrous events or signs occur. Mary pondered over these concrete signs of the Spirit in her life and the life of her people, Israel. In a sense, she is a new Israel who, like the first one, wrestled with the angel of the Lord—and thereby received the name "Israel" (Gen 12:28). Mary, too, pondered over the God-events in her life. What do we mean by a concrete sign? "A sign is, first of all, a pledge given to guarantee a prophetic revelation" (B. Meyer, *Catholic Biblical Quarterly*, Vol. 26, 1964, p. 39)—(e.g., Jer 44:29; Ez 4:3). In Luke "the sign is meant to set events in motion, to speed the approach to the mystery, to fix the age of faith on a scene portending salvation." The mystery is always what is intended; it is the object to be pondered, contemplated and penetrated. Mary, therefore, in her prayer, "kept with great concern all these events in her heart" (Lk 2:51). Notice that Mary is not "wondering" or "being amazed"— she is pondering, interpreting and turning over in her heart and memory the meaning of God's salvific action among her people. Mary is calm and probably joyful in pondering over in her heart these events, while those who wonder what manner of child this will be (Lk 1:65f) are not in the same prayerful attitude and disposition as Mary.

The word used for pondering over or treasuring is important in our understanding of how we are to pray biblically after the manner of Mary. In the overall context of wisdom literature it means "retention," "the keeping (of something) in mind" with the connotation of keeping (it) to oneself or of keeping it to ponder. Mary, as a Jewess who prays, makes the effort to plumb the meaning of God's revelation in the Torah, or his wisdom, his prophecy, discourse and his paradoxes. From the moment that Mary is introduced in the Annunciation Narrative she is presented as a person who attempts to fathom the mysteries of God within her and those which surround her. She is a reflective person; her prayer is a prayer of biblical reflection. In the first instance, she is reflecting upon the meaning of her Son who is Savior and Messiah-Lord. She doesn't solve the mystery; she ponders, attempts to understand, she "re-members" the events. Luke has set aside the second use of this phrase at the end of the Infancy Narrative. It acts as both a conclusion for the narrative and a transition to what will come in the future. Just as Mary is a bridge to the rest of the Gospel, her prayer stance of "pondering with concern" is one that we, as believers, should take to understand the beginnings of salvation and the workings of salvation in the person of Jesus the Lord.

LUKE'S GOSPEL: THE PRAYERFUL RESPONSE OF DISCIPLESHIP

Luke's texts on discipleship emphasize the need for wholesome response to the call of Jesus. The radical nature of discipleship is brought out together with the need for daily response through prayer and continuous perseverance.

The earliest response of Mary, the perfect disciple, occurs at the Annunciation—"Behold! the handmaid of the Lord; be it done to me according to thy word" (Lk 1:38). She is the joyful disciple of the Lord: "My spirit finds joy in God my Savior" (Lk 1:46).

Attention rests on the disciples' relationship to Jesus and his mission. Luke has written to persuade the disciples of Jesus to labor perseveringly in the apostolate of bringing the good news to all peoples. We have seen how Mary, as the perfect disciple, is present from the first moment of Jesus' life within her to his birth, presentation and finding in the temple. We see her during his ministry, and she is the bridge from his death to the birth of the Church after his resurrection and ascension (Acts 1:14).

We have seen how prayer is important in Luke's concept of discipleship. Mary, the perfect disciple, prays in a community, she prays reflecting and pondering over the word of God, and she prays within her Jewish tradition through the words of her Magnificat. Jesus' disciples had asked him to teach them how to pray and they are given the Lord's Prayer. There is a freshness about Luke's message. For that reason and especially for the fact that it presents such a variety of scenes in which Mary is present, I see it as a Gospel which can help us to understand our need for fidelity and loyalty. Here is a brief glimpse into the "joyful mysteries" as Luke presents them:

Annunciation	—	The response of Yes, single-heartedness of Mary.
Visitation	—	Love for her neighbor which integrates our love through its relational challenge.
Birth of Jesus	—	The fruitfulness of a life dedicated to God.
Presentation	—	The sword of sorrow/aloneness is ours in the shadow of the cross.

Finding of Jesus — God is ever close by even when we
in the Temple   think we have lost him.

A GLANCE AT THE WHOLE CANVAS—
THE SEQUENCE OF MARIAN TEXTS IN LUKE

1. The Call of Mary (Annunciation) 1:26–38

2. Mary visits Elizabeth 1:39–45

   • Elizabeth praises Mary 1:42–45

3. The Song of Mary 1:46–55

4. The Birth of Jesus 2:1–20

   • Jesus is born of Mary   1–7
   • The Shepherds   8–20

5. Naming of Jesus and Purification of Mary 2:21–40

6. The Finding in the Temple 2:41–52

7. Mary in the Public Ministry of Jesus

   Jesus' Family 8:19–21

   A Beatitude of Mary 11:27–28

8. Mary and the Community Acts 1:14

Discipleship Texts: Mary, a Disciple of Prayer: Lk 1:26–
   38; 2:19, 51; 11:1; Acts 1:14

Mary in John's Gospel

Discipleship Texts: John 13:1, 15, 17; 15:14–15; 13—17; 19:25–28
Mary Texts: John 2:1–12; 19:25–28a

THE GOSPEL OF JOHN

John's Gospel gives us the final portrait of Mary in the New Testament. This Gospel is the profound reflection of a Christian theologian-evangelist who was deeply rooted in the historical tradition of Jesus of Nazareth. For describing the image of Mary that he has given us, the sculptured figure of a woman who was the Mother of Jesus comes to mind. Only Michelangelo's Pietà would capture the mystery of this woman in such an art form—probably because it, too, was modeled on that marvelous image of Mary obtained from the fourth Gospel. John's Gospel presents a three-dimensional statue of Mary.

What texts have we in the fourth Gospel which relate to the Mother of Jesus? First, there are two scenes—the most significant passages—in which the Mother of Jesus appears:

(1) at the wedding feast of Cana, 2:1–12;
(2) at the foot of the cross, 19:25–27.

Then there are secondary or implicit references: John 1:13; 6:42; 7:41–43; 8:41—the virginal conception—and 2:12; 7:1–10—the brothers of Jesus. One striking feature in this Gospel is that she is never named personally as Mary. Her sole designation is as the Mother of Jesus or Woman.

The Gospel is literally composed of two parts: chapters 1–12, called the "Book of Signs," and chapters 13–20 (21), called the "Book of Glory."

The "Book of Signs" contains seven of the miracles of Jesus and discourses of Jesus which usually are confrontative toward those in leadership positions who refuse to hear his words. John prefers the term "sign" to miracle or prodigy, for he clearly wants all who believe in Jesus to get beyond miracles to the person of Jesus. The signs are merely means to this belief in him.

The "Book of Glory" consists in the final sections of the Gospel where Jesus reveals his "glory" to his intimate friends, his disciples. Even the Passion Narrative and Jesus' death on the cross is seen as a royal road and as an uplifting to his glory beside the Father.

From the passages wherein the Mother of Jesus appears or is inferred, we notice that all but one pertains to the Book of Signs. The two most important scenes, Cana and Calvary, however, complement each other. John makes use of the literary technique of inclusion to interpret the meaning of Mary in these scenes.

Let us now take a look at the passages of import in chapters 1–12.

The Prologue

John 1:1–18 is a hymn which serves as an overture to the entire Gospel. Some scholars, mostly Roman Catholic, have found verse 13 having significance for the role of

95

Mary in the conception of Jesus. "These are they who believe in his name—who were begotten not by blood, nor by carnal desire, nor by man's willing it, but by God." If we take the verse in its context, it pertains to that part of the prologue overture which contrasts the unbelieving world (Jn 1:11): "To his own he came, yet his own did not accept him," with those who believe in the word, and, therefore, in Jesus (Jn 1:12–13): "Any who did accept him he empowered to become children of God." The verse would then be characteristic of the most intimate friends of Jesus who appear in the second part of John's Gospel, the Book of Glory, John 13—21, contrasted with those unbelievers who generally appear in the Book of Signs, John 1—12.

In the most ancient and best of the Greek manuscripts, the reading for verse 13 is plural: "those who were begotten"; however, one old Latin MS and the following Christian writers attest to the singular: "he who was begotten"—Tertullian, Ambrose, and Augustine and the *Latin* versions of Irenaeus and Origen use the singular. These are great Christian believers and leaders. But we must notice that there is no evidence in the Koine Greek of John's text for such a singular reading which places a great burden of inauthenticity on the singular reading— for all of its witnesses are from the Latin or Western tradition and not from the more primitive and convincing Greek tradition. The meaning of the text implies that believers are begotten by God—a theme attested to in the first Epistle of John (1 Jn 3:9; 4:7; 5:1–4; 5:18a; Jn 3:3–8).

The great Johannine scholar, Sir Edwyn Hoskins, maintained that the plural was the original reading but thought that the language was so phrased as to recall the virgin birth of Jesus. However, the most recent ecumenical study of this text by scholars has opted to see no reference whatsoever to the conception of Jesus. I accept their opinion for two reasons: 1. The manuscripts are weighted to choose the plural. 2. The context seems to demand a plural referring to "believers" and not to the Word or Jesus. How fascinating it is even to explore the possibility of a reference to Mary in the Prologue. But we continually are presented with the evidence that the hymn is entirely Christological centering on the Word. It is, however, our task at hand to look at one of the most symbolic and remarkable scenes of all four Gospels—the wedding feast of Cana.

CANA: THE FIRST SIGN OF JESUS
AND JOHN'S FIRST IMAGE OF MARY

This first "sign" of Jesus in the fourth Gospel is placed on the seventh day of the occurrences that have been narrated from the moment John the Baptist enters the Gospel in Jn 1:19. Thus the Cana event climaxes, in a symbolic fashion, the new creation that Jesus has begun. The wedding feast *sign* is therefore a new sabbath in which the glory of God will be manifested in Jesus, his ambassador or apostle, and, as a result, his disciples are led to believe in him as a person. The appearance of the mother of Jesus occurs in the first line of the scene and her role is essential to the deeper level of understanding and interpretation which is the characteristic of the fourth evangelist. The personages are important: there is the "Mother of Jesus," Jesus himself at the center-stage, and then the "disciples of Jesus," including of course the beloved disciple.

Verse three indicates the crisis of having no wine. It is the Mother of Jesus who speaks for the first time in this scene and she addresses Jesus, saying to him, "They have no wine."

In verse four, the reply of Jesus goes beyond the immediate concern of Mary and the situation to the meaning of Jesus' *hour*—one of the great themes in the fourth Gospel. For John "hour" means the passion, death, and glorious resurrection of Jesus. Jesus then is telling his Mother that his true hour of glorification has not yet come. We are alerted for the first time to the great significance of his passing from this life to the Father in that "hour." Jesus also addresses his Mother as "Woman." This title is never used by a son in reference to his mother except in the fourth Gospel. John wants us and his community to understand the meaning of such an address when he will use it again.

It is precisely the dialogue between Jesus and his Mother which causes the greatest difficulty for scholars looking at these verses. How is it that there is apparently a rejection of Mary's intervention and yet a follow-through acceding to her request? Scholars answer this by positing layers within the composition of the narrative. The dialogue contains words which are theologically important for the evangelist. If we leave out the dialogue, Mary emerges as a believer in Jesus her Son who is at the same time a wonder-worker. If we leave the dialogue in, then she is the catalyst who enables Jesus to reveal the truest meaning of his life to his disciples—the glorification at the "hour" determined by the Father.

Biblical scholars Father Raymond Brown and B. Linders see the possibility of a pre-ministry "hidden-life" story somewhat akin to Luke's 2:41–51 (the finding in the temple) where Jesus astonishes the learned and his parents with his wisdom. If so, we have another witness to the pluralistic traditions surrounding the family of Jesus;

here, unlike in Mark, they are favorable to Jesus and his power.

The primary purpose of the scene is Christological, not Mariological. Contemporary Catholic scholarship is careful in not drawing devotional implications from the scene in reference to Mary. What has happened is that Jesus is attesting to his glory which comes exclusively from the Father:

> The Word became flesh and made his dwelling among us, and we have seen his glory; the glory of an only Son coming from the Father filled with enduring love (Jn 1:14).

He had promised his disciples such signs:

> Jesus responded, "Do you believe just because I told you I saw you under the fig tree? You will see much greater things than that" (Jn 1:50).

Looking at the term "woman" we are aware that John uses it in 4:21 for the Samaritan, in 8:10 for the adulteress (though this is not part of the authentic Johannine Gospel) and in 21:13 for Mary Magdalene. Thus John, too, could be attesting the fact that Jesus (just as in Mark's Gospel and to a lesser extent in Matthew's) attaches no special importance to the physical motherhood of Mary. The fact that in our pericope John calls her four times the Mother of Jesus seems to imply no playing down of the role, but we need the scene at the foot of the cross to make clear why in John's Gospel she is truly "mother"—namely, because she set the criterion of discipleship (belief in Jesus and the following of Jesus even to his death on the cross). An observation made by the ecumenical task force in *Mary in the New Testament* is:

Despite the problems of verses 3–5, we should not ex-
aggerate the negative side of the picture of the mother
of Jesus. The very fact that Jesus finally does supply the
wine requested makes it virtually impossible to maintain that the scene contains a harsh polemic against
his mother (*op. cit.*, p. 193).

John 2:12

This verse helps us to reflect upon the tradition of Jesus and "his brothers." It is also a verse which is quite interesting from the evidence of the manuscripts. I
personally think the summary statement on p. 196 of
Mary in the New Testament is quite descriptive of what
we could say about its meaning:

> One could put Mark and John together and postulate
> an early tradition that at the beginning of Jesus' min-
> istry his separation from his family was a deliberate ac-
> tion on his part, that they came to Capernaum to try
> to hold onto him, but recognized eventually that his
> calling had separated him from them, and that hence-
> forth they remained at Nazareth while he traversed
> Galilee and Judea.

John 6:42

> Is not this Jesus, the son of Joseph, whose father and
> mother we know?

Here John has this off-the-cuff remark from the dis-
believers. It is helpful, for it puts John in line with the tradition that Joseph was the legal father of Jesus (cf. Mt
1:16–17, 18–25; chapter 2; Lk 2:41–52). Once again it is
an example of the Johannine technique of misunderstanding, where Jesus speaks on one level, but the listener hears
on a lower, banal level.

Church beliefs divide most students on this line. Some see in it a misunderstanding of the virginal conception, others a direct denial of it. In reality, neither position is affirmed nor denied nor even centered upon by the evangelist. His concern is simply to contrast the spiritual with the purely physical connotations that the listeners are involved in. The situation is parallel to the Nicodemus account and his misunderstanding. Certainly, the later refined doctrines of the Church are not in the intention of John, even in seed-form. "All that we can be sure of from 6:42 is that human parentage is no obstacle to divine origins (cf. 1:45 'son of Joseph' from Nazareth)" (*ibid.*, p. 198).

John 7:1–10: The Unbelieving Brothers of Jesus

As in 2:12, so here the brothers are kept separate from the disciples. As in Mark, his brothers are basically unconvinced about Jesus. Their request has a certain parallel to Cana, yet seems to be more of a sarcastic, frivolous taunting of Jesus. It is in this scene that we no longer meet up with the brothers of Jesus. As unbelievers John dismisses them from his pages; however, Mary will appear once more as a believer at the foot of the cross.

John 7:41–43: Is Not the Messiah from Bethlehem?

Once again, we have an example of misunderstanding on the part of unbelievers. John speaks on a higher level for the believers; for the non-Christian reader and listener only the literal facts mean anything—and often lead to nothing for them. John is *ironic*. He is not going against the evidence of the rest of the New Testament that Jesus is a Davidid (Paul, Mark, Matthew, Luke, pastorals, Revelation—with Christological implications). We must, however, remember that John's Christological emphasis is very different from the Synoptics and Paul. For him Jesus is the pre-existent Word who is one with the Father before all creation came to be.

John 8:41: Born of Fornication

This is one of the verses cited as evidence for a Jewish charge that Jesus' birth was illegitimate. Thus the verse is asserted by some scholars/believers as a reference to the virginal conception (Mt 1:18–20). If illegitimacy is meant, it is quite subtle because we have just seen in 6:41 that they think Jesus' father is Joseph. It is not his human parentage but his divine origin which is under attack in chapter eight.

John 19:25–27: The Mother at the Foot of the Cross

The Book of Glory deals with the intimate relationship of Jesus with his own (Jn 13:1). The fact that Mary appears in the most climatic scene in the drama of the passion and death of Jesus demonstrates that she is considered a disciple of Jesus at that most solemn moment. She is present, standing with the disciple whom Jesus loved; they are entrusted to one another; the community of the beloved disciple is born and the mother of Jesus— the Woman of faith—is present.

This scene is in the center of the rapid symbolic events which unfold near the cross of Jesus. John presents four women at the foot of the cross. What we remember from the Synoptics is a tradition of three women (Mk 15:40; Mt 27:56; Lk 23:49). John has created a heightened dramatic portrayal of the scene and has given a greater role to Mary, the Mother of Jesus, than do the Synoptics. Her presence there shows her to be of importance to the Johannine community.

Several times within his Gospel, John has presented

a pattern of seven scenes which either parallel one another or present an ascent to the main event. We saw how
seven such events are hinted at in the very first chapters
of this Gospel when John builds up the call of the disciples
to the revelation of Jesus' glory on the seventh day at the
wedding feast of Cana; now as the life of Jesus closes,
seven scenes are again presented by the evangelist. There
were also parallel scenes in the trial of Jesus with Pilate—
seven such where Jesus is brought in and taken out to the
praetorium in seven succeeding situations.

The same is true now that we have come to the greatest sign in this Gospel—the death of Jesus on the Cross.
Both Father R. Brown and Father G. Montague more recently have pointed out the Chiastic ascent from 19:16–
19:42. Both scholars tell us that Jesus gives his mother to
the beloved disciple in the most important of these
scenes. Here is the arrangement Montague provides:

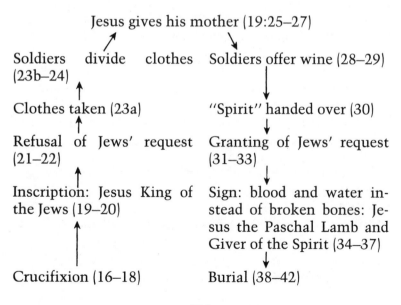

Jesus gives his mother (19:25–27)

Soldiers divide clothes (23b–24) Soldiers offer wine (28–29)

Clothes taken (23a) "Spirit" handed over (30)

Refusal of Jews' request (21–22) Granting of Jews' request (31–33)

Inscription: Jesus King of the Jews (19–20) Sign: blood and water in-
stead of broken bones: Je-
sus the Paschal Lamb and
Giver of the Spirit (34–37)

Crucifixion (16–18) Burial (38–42)

103

(Symbolic meaning shown through Chiastic structure which centers upon 19:25–27)

> Near the cross of Jesus there stood his mother, his mother's sister, Mary, the wife of Clopas, and Mary Magdalene. Seeing his mother there with the disciple whom he loved, Jesus said to his mother, "Woman, there is your son." In turn, he said to the disciple, "There is your mother." From that hour onward, the disciple took her into his care. After that, Jesus realizing that everything was now finished said to fulfill the Scripture, "I am thirsty."

The point George Montague makes in his excellent article is that we can understand our relationship to Mary through this Calvary scene if we interpret it correctly. "God consecrates us through giving us Mary as mother, and we are consecrated by receiving that gift (a gift which means, as it did for the beloved disciple, the person of Mary and a concrete community)" (Marianist Resources Commission, Vol. 12, 1 doc. 63, February 1981, p. 10). "For the beloved disciple to 'take' Mary into his responsibility was to accept the entire community which Jesus, from the Cross, was confiding to the disciple. In a similar way and in perfect continuity with this scene, we simultaneously accept the mother of Jesus into our lives and take unto ourselves that community of which she is the mother and the central figure" (*ibid.*, p. 1).

You recall how at Cana the beginnings of Jesus' hour—his passion, death, and resurrection and his return to the Father—were begun through the initiative of the "Mother of Jesus" who was addressed by Jesus as "Woman." Here the hour has come and is being accomplished with Jesus freely giving his Mother to the beloved disciple while again addressing her as "Woman." The

Cana scene mirrors the Calvary scene. What was promised is fulfilled, what was foreshadowed and anticipated is brought to accomplishment and conclusion. Jesus has changed water into an abundance of messianic wine; now he gives the gift of his Mother to the beloved disciple while pouring forth his Spirit—testified by the blood and water which flow from his side (Jn 19:34). The Christian community is born as Jesus dies breathing his Spirit upon the two most precious loved ones: his Mother and his beloved disciple.

The great scholar R. Bultmann saw an image of the Church and synagogue in this climactic event. Mary for him represented what was Judaism while the beloved disciple represented Christianity. The image is helpful, but Mary and the beloved disciple are united through the Spirit of Jesus and they form the community of Jesus which we call the Church.

In a creative article on the Mariology of the fourth Gospel, Juan Alfaro, O.S.B. shows us that the whole of John's Gospel proceeds in a chiastic structure. In his own structure Alfaro shows us that the second section of the gospel—let us call it "a"—is designated: The renewal: Cana, purification of the temple, 2:1–25; it is paralleled at the end by Calvary or "b"—The new order: the process of Jesus and Calvary, John 19:1—19:42. Alfaro helps us understand our relationship to Mary for he says, "The narration of Calvary describes the birth of a new community, a new Chosen People, a Messianic family, united in the same faith, under the care and protection of a common mother, vivified by the Spirit and sharing the same sacraments. This new community receives the blessings promised to Israel and will be witness of the revelation of the glory of Jesus and of the love of God for the world" (p. 5).

105

By the fact that this is the only Marian scene in this portion of John's Gospel, called the "Book of Glory," it has a clarity and importance as an event which shows us once more Mary as the perfect disciple. This entire book centers on the love, care, and concern Jesus has for "his own," especially his beloved disciples who now are called his brothers and, of course, Mary his mother. According to *Mary in the New Testament,* "To introduce the mother of Jesus into this atmosphere is to bring her into the context of discipleship" (*op. cit.,* p. 206).

We also have to remember that the four women who are mentioned in this scene are with Jesus as he is dying on the cross. In the other Gospels, the women are mentioned only after the death of Jesus. They are said to be *apo makrothen*—distant from the place of crucifixion—while in John these disciples of the Lord are *para to stauro*—near or close by the cross. Therefore, this shows more the situation of true discipleship—bearing or being near the cross each day.

Even if this scene were not historical—but I believe it is—"the presence of the mother of Jesus and the beloved disciple reflects Johannine inventiveness that may enhance the importance of Mary for the Johannine community; the evangelist would scarcely have created a central crucifixion scene if it did not have significance. . . . In this Calvary scene at the foot of the cross Jesus gives his physical mother a spiritual role as mother of the disciple par excellence and the disciple a role as the son" (*ibid.,* pp. 210, 213). This scene is preceded by a revelatory word in John's Gospel—*Now, Behold* (1:29, 36, 47).

JOHN'S GOSPEL:
THE DISCIPLESHIP OF THE BELOVED (13:1, 15, 17; 15:14–15; 13—
17; 19:25–28).

As the Book of Glory begins (Jn 13:1), Jesus openly reveals the depth of his love for his disciples:

> He had loved his own in this world, and would show his love for them to the end.

The entire farewell speech of Jesus (chapters 13—17) is a revelation of who Jesus is to his chosen ones, the disciples. The intimate relationship between himself and them is now spoken of in terms of friendship:

> You are my friends if you do what I command you. I no longer speak of you as slaves, for a slave does not know what his master is about. Instead, I call you friends, since I have made known to you all that I heard from my Father (Jn 15:14–15).

The conditions for such friendship and discipleship are living out the words and love-commands of Jesus. Jesus tells his disciples:

> I give you a new commandment: love one another; as I have loved you, so you are to love one another. If there is this love among you, then all will know that you are my disciples (13:34–35, New English Bible).

Mary understood what it means to love Jesus in this intimate manner, both as his mother and as his disciple. The first appearance of Mary at the wedding feast of Cana marked the beginnings of Jesus' revelation to his disciples and to her as a woman led to the fullness of belief:

107

> Thus did he reveal his glory, and his disciples believed
> in him (Jn 2:11).

At Cana it was Mary who gave to the servants those insightful words which are now understood by all of Jesus' disciples, "Do whatever he tells you" (Jn 2:5). Though she is not mentioned as being present at the farewell address of Jesus, she did understand and experience the call to humble service. Jesus through the washing of the feet of his disciples gives them an explicit action-command of love:

> What I just did was to give you an example: as I have
> done, so you must do. . . . Once you know all these
> things, blest will you be if you put them into practice
> (Jn 13:15, 17).

Mary's presence at the foot of the cross attests to her love and commitment to Jesus, her Son. Standing with the beloved disciple, she receives the love of Jesus and listens to his final words of revelation. Jesus, too, realizes that his journey to the Father has been completed, for after giving Mary to the beloved disciple, the evangelist tells us:

> After that, Jesus, realizing that everything was now
> finished . . . bowed his head and delivered over his
> spirit" (Jn 19:28, 30).

The fullness of his life is now received by the two disciples standing beneath the cross. Mary and the beloved disciple represent all of us as they witness the beginning of the community: the Church is brought forth from the cross and the life-giving water which flows from the side of Christ (baptism) and his blood, representing the Eucharist. These two disciples are symbols of the call to perfect discipleship, which reaches its highest demands in the context of community and the care and concern we have for one another. Mary, as the perfect disciple, is presented always in terms of her relationship to the community—either to the community of Israel and its fulfillment in Jesus at Cana, or to the Christian community and its fulfillment at Calvary through the gift of Mary to the beloved disciple. Intimacy, love, community and mutual sharing are presented at the event at the foot of the cross. Discipleship began as a new creation at Cana through the sign of water made into wine, while at Calvary sign becomes *event* in the commitment of love given by the Spirit of Jesus to his mother and the beloved disciple.

Discipleship in the fourth Gospel reaches the heights of Jesus' revelation because it takes on the characteristics of an intimate relationship with Jesus. We are no longer servants nor even disciples—we are brothers and sisters in Jesus. The male hero of the Johannine community is called the "beloved disciple." I think he represents us as living out the fullness of our Christian life with wholesomeness. This Gospel, more than the other three, shows us what discipleship is once we have "our act together" or once we have worked out what we had to and we have it all together.

8

Revelation and Mary
and Early Biblical Reflections

Mary Texts: Revelation 11:19—12:17

This final chapter consists of two parts which bring our study of Mary to a conclusion. The first part treats the last possible reference to Mary as a symbol of the believing disciples or the Church (Revelation 11:19—12:17); the second section is a presentation of the three earliest Church leaders who reflected upon Mary as she emerges from the Bible for them. These writers are Ignatius of Antioch, Justin the Martyr, and Irenaeus of Lyons. These saintly men are our closest contact with Mary after the pages of the New Testament. By including them we are able to see how Mary was considered in relationship to Christ from the time of the New Testament to the year 200 A.D.

The final text which appears in the Book of Revelation may have a symbolic presentation of Mary as an image of the Church. It reads:

> Then the sanctuary of God in heaven opened, and the ark of the covenant could be seen inside it. Then came flashes of lightning, peals of thunder and an earthquake, and violent hail.

Now a great sign appeared in heaven: a woman,
adorned with the sun, standing on the moon, and with
the twelve stars on her head for a crown. She was pregnant, and in labor, crying aloud in the pangs of child-
birth. Then a second sign appeared in the sky, a huge
red dragon which had seven heads and ten horns, and
each of the seven heads crowned with a coronet. Its tail
dragged a third of the stars from the sky and dropped
them to the earth, and the dragon stopped in front of
the woman as she was having the child, so that he
could eat it as soon as it was born from its mother. The
woman brought a male child into the world, the son
who was to rule all the nations with an iron sceptre,
and the child was taken straight up to God and to his
throne, while the woman escaped into the desert,
where God had made a place of safety ready, for her
to be looked after in the twelve hundred and sixty
days. . . .

As soon as the devil found himself thrown down to the
earth, he sprang in pursuit of the woman, the mother
of the male child, but she was given a huge pair of eagle's wings to fly away from the serpent into the desert,
to the place where she was to be looked after for a year
and twice a year and half a year. So the serpent vomited
water from his mouth, like a river, after the woman, to
sweep her away in the current, but the earth came to
her rescue; it opened its mouth and swallowed the
river thrown up by the dragon's jaws. Then the dragon
was enraged with the woman and went away to make
war on the rest of her children, that is, all who obey
God's commandments and bear witness for Jesus (Rev
11:19—12:6; 12:13–17).

Is Mary symbolically depicted in chapter 12 of the
Book of Revelation (the Apocalypse) as the woman

clothed with the sun and the moon beneath her feet? Serious efforts in scholarship offer both a yes and a no answer.

From the historical-critical method, Revelation 12 can be seen as part of a work written to address a Christian community undergoing intense persecution at the end of the first century. The writing is apocalyptic and highly symbolic; this literary genre was well known to the Judaeo-Christian milieu (it is strongly reflected in the Dead Sea Scrolls as well) and suited the psychological situation of the people who were in need of strengthening, reassurance, warning and direction in how to create a meaning in the light of faith for what they were experiencing at the hands of Roman persecution.

From the religious imagery embedded in the Hebrew Scriptures, the woman is a symbol of both the Old and the New Israel. The former has brought forth the Messiah who has been taken up to heaven, while the latter, the Church, experiences both persecution and the sustaining providence of God:

> As soon as the devil found himself thrown down to the earth, he sprang in pursuit of the woman, the mother of the male child, but she was given a huge pair of eagle's wings to fly away from the serpent into the desert, to the place where she was to be looked after for a year and twice a year and half a year.

Sources for such imagery flow from both canonical and inspired Scriptures (Gen 3:15; 6:1–4) as well as the apocryphal works (1 Enoch 6–19, Jubilees 5; Adam and Eve 12–17). The center section of Revelation 12, namely vv. 7–9, stem from the Jewish myth of the fall of the evil angels from heaven:

And now war broke out in heaven, when Michael with his angels attacked the dragon. The dragon fought back with his angels, but they were defeated and driven out of heaven. The great dragon, the primeval serpent, known as the devil or Satan, who had deceived all the world, was hurled down to the earth and his angels were hurled down with him (Rev 12:7–9).

At another level this symbolic scene is easily *accommodated* and read in terms of Mary as the woman, since the combination of Old and New Israel and the giving birth to the child who is the Messiah (*ho Christos*) (cf. Ps 2:9) who is Jesus are easily applied to the Mother of the Messiah:

Then I saw some thrones, and I saw those who are given the power to be judges take their seats on them. I saw the souls of all who had been beheaded for having witnessed for Jesus and for having preached God's word, and those who refused to worship the beast or his statue and would not have the brand-mark on their foreheads or hands; they came to life, and reigned with Christ for a thousand years (Rev 20:4).

Mary as woman is the archetype of the Church and the full flowering of the Old Israel. As archetype of the Church she is a sign that the Church is surrounded by God's power and protection ("clothed with the sun"), is in continuity with the past people of God, yet suggestive of the new people (the significance of the twelve stars for the patriarchs and apostles), and, like that older people, is led into the desert where God nourishes her (suggestive of the manna) and bears her up on eagle's wings (Dt 32:10–11).

Since the scene is so symbolical, the interpretation of

113

chapter 12 has to be more than one that relies on the historical-critical method. I would suggest that the method of structural exegesis or the semiotic method can give us new insights which are based on the text itself and on a careful observation of the symbolic elements present within the scenes. For example, the text lends itself to the following topographical "square":

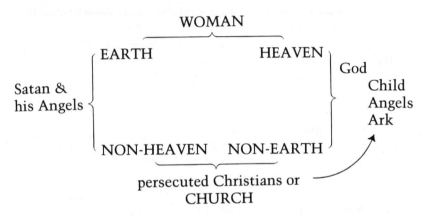

WOMAN

EARTH HEAVEN God

Satan &   Child
his Angels   Angels
            Ark

NON-HEAVEN NON-EARTH

persecuted Christians or
CHURCH

The woman appears on the heavenly area but is hidden on earth. She spans both as a heavenly and as an earthly reality. She is on the side of the divine heavenly reality that includes the divine court, the ark, the child and God's angels. (In Mary's going up to see Elizabeth south of Jerusalem, David's going up to Jerusalem with the ark is echoed. The ark is a symbol of God's presence.)

The dragon is opposite all this as opposed to God; it is excluded from heaven. The angels of Satan are non-heaven, likewise; that is, they are out of the sphere of goodness and totally in the realm where evil is enacted. The persecuted Christians are non-earth because they are children of the woman in heaven where their inheritance exists; but they have not yet achieved it and so they are non-heaven. They are related to the woman but are not totally protected from the rage of the dragon. The woman thus is an archetype of the Church which looks to her for a similar fulfillment in the heavens once the dragon is destroyed and persecution ceases. One can easily see how in the liturgy for the Assumption the symbolism is accommodated to the person of Mary.

A second attempt at creating an interpretative structure from the imagery of chapter 12 could lead the reader into a deeper insight:

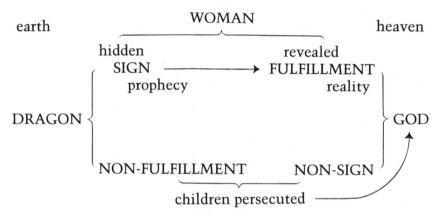

Here *sign* carries with it the meaning of the "already" but "not yet," the partially revealed, the limited reality, and the ultimate fulfillment and victory of God. The Church comes into its reward as the new Jerusalem that already has begun. God who is truth and is faithful has already won and kept his promise. The divine fullness of reality is present already in heaven where the heavenly court is moving on toward final triumph through the salvation of those who were being persecuted. The dragon is also a sign but symbolic of non-fulfillment, ultimate defeat and deception for all who believe and accept its rule or succumb to the threats of persecution. Siding with the forces of evil, untruth, chaos, disorder, and injustice lead to ultimate frustration and non-fulfillment. The children of the woman experience non-fulfillment now in the suffering of persecution. They are not a sign any more than God is, but they will through his saving victory enter into fulfillment which is the heavenly Jerusalem in its final triumph when all that is evil, deceptive, rebellious, like the sea and chaos will pass away.

> I saw the holy city, and the new Jerusalem, coming down from God out of heaven, as beautiful as a bride all dressed for her husband (Rev 21:2).

My reason for showing both the historical-critical method and the semiotic (structural analysis) of our passage in Revelation 12 is to present the objective discoveries of such interpretative methods. From a pastoral perspective, we could say that we have something in common with the era of a text that speaks about Domitian's persecution (81–96 A.D.). Many people are oppressed and are threatened by many networks of evil power that exercise injustice. We have to discover whether we are contributing to the works of injustice by oppressing the poor and helpless, the little ones of the woman. We also must have confidence that God is working out an ultimate victory for the oppressed. Mary, in an accommodated sense, is like the woman as a sign of hope and victory for the Church and the world. She, as we have seen in the Gospels, had the courage to believe and to persevere in following her Son Jesus despite inward struggles and outward opposition to him. She now is experiencing the fullness of life. The text does not stop with Mary as a disciple; it also encourages us to see ourselves as part of a people cared for by God even as we experience opposition to hostility. We are not alone in our discipleship to Jesus on either the human or the divine/heavenly level or dimension.

Mary as disciple is the faithful daughter of Sion; she expresses in her spiritual journey the best of Israel, the people of God and a community of faith awaiting the coming of the Messiah. She also is the first among believers in the new community of Christ who is made blessed because of her faith and her obedience to the Word of God become flesh. She also as a disciple witnesses to the mystery of suffering because of her testimony to her Son Jesus.

IGNATIUS OF ANTIOCH'S MARIAN REFLECTIONS

Even while the New Testament was in the process of being formed, a leader of the Christian community at Antioch, Ignatius, wrote about the presence of Mary within the mystery of Christ. We are reminded by St. Luke in the Acts of the Apostles:

> It was at Antioch that the *disciples* were called *Christians* for the first time (Acts 11:29).

Ignatius wrote during the time of the emperor Trajan (98–117 A.D.). His only extant letters are the seven which were penned during his journey from Antioch to Rome where he was martyred.

In his letter to the Ephesians (7:2) he describes the divinity and humanity of Jesus in these terms:

> There is one Physician, who is both flesh and spirit, born and not born, who is God in man, true life in death, both from Mary and from God, first able to suffer and then unable to suffer, Jesus Christ our Lord.

Near the end of the same letter his most important words about Mary are:

117

For our God, Jesus Christ, was conceived by Mary in accord with God's plan: of the seed of David, it is true, but also of the Holy Spirit. He was born and was baptized so that by his submission he might purify the water. . . . The virginity of Mary, her giving birth, and also the death of the Lord, were hidden from the prince of this world: three mysteries loudly acclaimed, but wrought in the silence of God.

His writing to the Smyrnaeans 1:1 confirms the fact that he believed in the reality of Jesus' birth from the virgin Mary:

You are fully persuaded concerning our Lord, that he is in truth of the family of David according to the flesh, Son of God by the will and power of God, truly born of a virgin.

His final reference to Mary in Trallians (9:1) emphasizes the Davidic lineage of Jesus (just as we saw in Matthew's Gospel).

Be deaf therefore when anyone speaks to you apart from Jesus Christ, of David's lineage, of Mary, who was truly born and ate and drank, was truly persecuted under Pontius Pilate, was truly crucified and died in the sight of those in heaven and on earth and in the underworld, who was truly raised from the dead when his Father raised him up. And in this same manner his Father will raise us up in Christ Jesus, if we believe in him without whom we have no hope.

From what we have studied in the Gospels and Epistles of St. Paul, we can see that Ignatius combined and conflated the texts of the New Testament in his reflections on Mary. He felt free to do this as the leader of his Christian community.

JUSTIN THE MARTYR'S REFLECTIONS ON MARY

The next early Church leader who has commented on Mary through a use of the Scriptures is St. Justin, the martyr (100/110—165 A.D.). He was a convert who lived at Nablus, Samaria. An astute philosopher (a Stoic, Pythagorean, Peripatetic and Platonist), he wrote prolifically but only two or three of his writings survive—the "Apologies" and "Dialogue with Trypho the Jew."

In his "Dialogue" Justin surpasses his predecessors by using scriptural texts to prove Scripture and by emphasizing the argument from prophecy. He eagerly presents exhaustive proof of the validity of the Scriptures and of his own validity as a Christian philosopher. Justin always considers the Hebrew Scriptures (Old Testament) as a part of his Christian heritage and uses the Old Testament personalities and events as part of his Christian heritage. To him as much as to any other Christian apologist and Church Father we may owe it that the Gospel has remained rooted in the religion of the Old Testament, and, on one basis or another, has not been unfriendly to human thought.

In Marian thought, he is the first Christian author who adds a counterpoint to the Pauline parallel: Christ-Adam, by contrasting Mary with Eve.

Since it is written of Him in the memoirs of the Apostles that He is the Son of God, and since we call Him Son, we have understood that before all creatures He proceeded from the Father by His will and power—for in the words of the Prophets He is addressed in one way or another as Wisdom and Day and East and Sword and Stone and Rod and Jacob and Israel—and that He became Man by the Virgin so that the course which was

119

taken by disobedience in the beginning through the agency of the serpent, might be also the course by which it would be put down. For Eve, a virgin and undefiled, conceived the word of the serpent, and bore disobedience and death. But the Virgin Mary received faith and joy when the angel Gabriel announced to her the glad tidings that the Spirit of the Lord would come upon her and the power of the Most High would overshadow her, for which reason the Holy One being born of her is the Son of God. And she replied: "Be it done unto me according to thy word" (Luke 1:30) (Dialogue with Trypho the Jew, 100).

We see how Justin considers the Gospels as "Memoirs of the Lord" rather than as "writings" (Scripture). He is remembering the words and events of Jesus more by heart than from a written New Testament.

In his First Apology, he comments on Isaiah 7:14 which we have seen is present in Matthew 1:23:

And again, hear how Isaiah expressly foretold that He (Jesus) was to be born of a virgin. He states the following: "Behold, a virgin shall conceive and bear a son; and for His name they shall say 'God-with-us.' " The phrase "Behold, a virgin shall conceive" means, certainly, that the virgin shall conceive without intercourse. For if she has intercourse with anyone at all, she would not be a virgin. But the power of God, coming upon the virgin, overshadowed her, and caused her, while yet a virgin, to conceive (First Apology, 30).

IRENAEUS OF LYONS' REFLECTIONS ON MARY

The final early writer I wish to present in this book is Irenaeus of Lyons (140–220 A.D.). Irenaeus is the most important interpreter of the Scriptures in the second century. He probably is from Smyrna in Asia Minor and in his early youth had listened to the sermons of St. Polycarp.

It is Irenaeus who first gives Mary an identity of her own that sets her as a new Eve, an image of the Church, and a special cause in the history of salvation. Through typological comparisons (Adam-Christ, Eve-Mary) and prophetic statements (Is 7:14), Irenaeus asserts the messiahship of Jesus. He reads the Isaiah prophecy as a sure sign of the virginal conception and birth and as a sign of the true humanity of Jesus.

Here is an example of how he writes about Mary:

> And if the former (Eve) did disobey God, yet the latter (Mary) was persuaded to be obedient to God, in order that the Virgin Mary might become the advocate of the virgin Eve. And thus, as the human race fell bondage to a death by means of a virgin, so it is rescued by a virgin, virginal disobedience having been balanced in the opposite scale by virginal obedience (Against Heresies 5.19.1).

Moreover, on interpreting Mary, Irenaeus rests on the shoulders of the giants who have gone before him. Not only does he depend on the inspired writers of the Old Testament, but also upon his immediate forerunner, Justin the martyr. In chapter nineteen of Book Three, *Against Heresies*, he uses the same scriptural passages and a similar development as Justin's use of texts to confirm his understanding of Isaiah 7:14. (He and Justin cite Isaiah 53:8, Jeremiah 17:9, and Matthew 16:16 for Justin's use of Matthew 11:27.)

Irenaeus makes use of St. Paul's letters (Phil 2:8; Rom 5:12–19) to demonstrate how we are totally united to Christ (his word is "recapitulated") because of his birth from the Virgin Mary and his resurrection:

He (Christ) recapitulated in himself what was shaped of old. As through one man's disobedience sin had gained entrance, and death had obtained power as a result, so through the obedience of one man righteousness was introduced and has caused life to flourish in men previously dead. And as Adam was first made from untilled soil and received his being from virgin earth (since God had not yet sent rain and man had not yet cultivated the ground) and was fashioned by the hand of God (that is, by the Word of God "by whom all things were made . . .") so he who existed as the Word, recapitulating in himself Adam, received from Mary, who was still a virgin, a birth befitting this recapitulation of Adam (Against Heresies 3.21.10).

One would profit in reading his third and fifth book of Against Heresies while looking for the typological comparisons he uses (Adam-Christ, Eve-Mary) to discover how he sees a relation between the Old and New Testaments. Irenaeus discerns a total plan of God at work through the two Testaments that will eventually lead to the fullness of self-revelation by the Father. The Holy Spirit has acted as the inspiring agency in the Prophets (especially) to foretell the coming of the promised Messiah and to point decisively to Jesus of Nazareth as that One. Major examples of the typological examples given by Irenaeus comprise: Mary as the new Eve, the Tree of Paradise and the Tree of the Cross, Adam and the recapitulation in Christ (the sacrifices and rituals of the old law and the Eucharist), transfiguration of the sabbath, Moses and his marriage to the Ethiopian as a type of the Church married to Christ and receiving even the pagans/Gentiles on an equal intimacy with the Jews, the exodus and the Passion of Christ as liberation, the water in the desert and the living waters of baptism, the temple as a figure of the new temple of the Church and the heavenly Jerusalem, the birth of Moses as a figure of the virginal conception, the conflict between Christians and Jews prefigured by the conflict with Esau, the wife of Lot turned into a pillar of salt as a type of the Church as salt of the earth.

CONCLUSION

Through this sketchy presentation of Irenaeus, we complete our book on Mary which has taken us from the pages of the New Testament up to the year 200 A.D. We have emphasized what the biblical texts say about her in relation to her Son and in the context of her discipleship.

This book has as its purpose to lay the foundations for a scriptural understanding of who the mother of Jesus is. What is said of her should help us to understand the history of Marian thought and devotion as it developed in the Church. It would also help us to test and discern what is most valuable in our tradition and how to eliminate with sensitivity and care those accidental accretions of the past in our devotion to the mother of Jesus while building up new forms of thought, exegesis, prayer and liturgical celebrations around the person of Mary.

We have come from the shadow of Mary in Paul's writings which showed us the Jewish atmosphere and background that surrounded her as a believing Jewess to the reverse side of that shadow in the bright symbolism of the Woman as sign and archetype of the Church in Revelation. We also saw how three early Christian leaders took the Scriptures and applied them to Mary the Virgin and the Woman of faith who is an image of who we are as Church.

Epilogue

Ever since Vatican II, Mary is present in a new way that is encouraging for each of us as disciples of Jesus. We now find her as she is in the Sacred Scriptures—a strong woman who is as human as we are. The liturgy also reminds us of her by referring to the same texts we have explored and explained in this book. In a sense, because of Vatican II we have become aware of relating to Mary through her discipleship. Without losing sight of her motherhood we now can see our own call as disciples reflected and witnessed in her life's journey with Jesus. Seeing her as our sister and as a disciple gives us an alternate approach to understanding her in today's Church. She offers us a spirituality that is realistic for our everyday life and one that resonates with the ordinary and insignificant tasks we share with her in our journey of faith. This prepares us for the larger responsibilities we have.

Mary also holds a key role in ecumenism—especially if the Catholic vision is to be understood, shared, and rendered reasonable to our brothers and sisters who share the same faith in her Son Jesus. In our everyday lives we would never neglect to acknowledge a friend's mother. Jesus' mother is a friend, too. As Christians we have to come to know the Jewishness of Jesus better because of Mary. She offers us the human context which is at the heart of Jesus' Jewishness. Today a Jew is known to be such by the fact that his mother is Jewish. It is no different for Jesus of Nazareth, son of Mary of Nazareth.

Today we are looking for leaders who offer us and our families a vision and hope. Mary the disciple and mother of Jesus is one of these leaders who offers us such a vision and hope. We have seen her through the eyes of the evangelists as a woman who always was faithfully free as a disciple of Jesus. As one of God's called (and we all are!) she offers us a sterling example of discipleship. Unlike Peter she doesn't falter or waver, yet she is as real and human as he. She never is put on a pedestal by the evangelists; rather, she emerges as a faithful disciple.

What I have written about Mary springs from my own devotion to her as a Marianist priest. I have experienced a close relationship to Mary throughout my life and have tried to deepen this relationship by prayer, study, and sharing what I know about her with others. In fact, the ideas in this book sprung from a workshop on Mary's presence in the Scriptures. I further developed the theme through a series of retreats for religious, for women, and for my own fellow Marianists. Because of my responsibilities, I was able to present the theme in Canada, Australia, and Africa. All were interested in hearing about Mary. Now I am grateful to so many people whom I met for giving many new insights which helped me in the writing of these chapters. I am sure some readers will recognize their contribution in the pages of this book.

I am also a member of a Christian-Jewish Dialogue group which was open to hearing about Mary of Nazareth. In fact, one of the Jewish members spoke for the group in a letter sent to me:

"I want to write down some of my reflections after participating in your most stimulating seminar on *Mary,*

125

the Disciple of Jesus or as I put it to most of my friends and acquaintances who said 'you went where?' 'To a workshop on *Mary, the Jewish Mother of Jesus.'*

". . . To continue with Mary—I had no trouble of course in perceiving her as a disciple. And I was very happy to have your clarification of exactly what is meant by disciple. I understand what a Talmida (disciple) is. Ani Talmida Ivrit (I am a Hebrew disciple)—for years now and I still don't know it. I shared with you already the burning question, 'Did the chassidim (pious dedicated Jews) borrow back the custom of following after the rebbe (rabbi) or is this still a hangover from early Rabbinic life?' When one is in Israel one feels transported back to medieval Poland when the chassidim come streaming out of Mea Shearim (a street in Jerusalem's orthodox sector) in groups following after their own rebbe in white capote and shtreimel (hat with brim). After this weekend that we studied together, I will always be reminded of Jesus, too, when I see them but with one important difference—his followers included *women* too.

"I have a topic for some future Christian Jewish Dialogue meeting: How does Mary fit the picture of the perfect wife and mother as presented in 'A Woman of Valor,' Proverbs 31, the poem that is recited proverbially each Shabbat (Sabbath) to the woman of the house? Haven't had time to analyze my own feelings about her yet to see if I perceive her that way, but I think it would be interesting. I could empathize with the person of Mary—you painted her as strong, like Deborah; fiercely maternal, like Rebecca; loyal, like Ruth; beautiful, like Rachel; patient, like Sarah (also pretty fiercely maternal); fervent in her religious ardor, like Miriam; faithful to the Lord, like Hannah."

126

I think this Jewishness of Jesus is important for us in understanding his human qualities. Mary is the person who brought him to us as a Jew. The relationship of a mother to her Son was deepened by a daily process of a new relationship which Jesus called her to experience—that of discipleship. As Christians we, too, are called to discipleship each day. Each Gospel gives us a different aspect of discipleship and Mary's role within it. I think these various images of Mary can help each of us relate to the paradigm of discipleship. What is exciting about the New Testament is that Mary of Nazareth is the first disciple of Jesus who enables us to experience the process of becoming a disciple at any stage of the call in which we find ourselves. Like those present at Cana we, too, can hear her saying to us: "Do whatever he tells you" (Jn 2:5).

Bibliography

MARY IN SPIRITUALITY AND PRAYER

Billy, Dennis J., C.SS.R. "The Marian Kernel." *Review for Religious* 43 (May–June, 1984), 415–420.

Breig, James. *Hail Mary: Woman, Wife, Mother of God.* Chicago: Claretian Publications, 1980.

Callahan, Sidney. *The Magnificat, the Prayer of Mary.* New York: Seabury Press, 1975.

Cameli, Louis J. *Mary's Journey.* New York: Sadlier, 1982.

Carretto, Carlo. *Blessed Are You Who Believed.* Maryknoll, N.Y.: Orbis Books, 1983.

Carroll, Eamon R., O. Carm. *Understanding the Mother of Jesus.* Wilmington, Del.: Michael Glazier, Inc., 1979.

Chervin, Ronda & Neill, Mary. *Bringing the Mother of God with You: Sources of Healing in Marian Meditation.* New York: Seabury Press, 1982.

Johnson, Ann. *Miryam of Nazareth: Woman of Strength and Wisdom.* Notre Dame, Ind.: Ave Maria Press, 1984.

Lynch, John W. *A Woman Wrapped in Silence.* New York: Paulist Press, 1975.

Maloney, George A., S.J. *Mary, the Womb of God.* Denville, N.J.: Dimension Books, 1976.

Neubert, Emil, S.M. *Our Gift from God.* Translated by Sylvester P. Juergens. Dayton, Ohio: Marianist Press, 1962.

Noone, Patricia, S.C. *Mary for Today.* Chicago: Thomas More Press, 1977.

O'Donnell, Christopher, O.Carm. *Life in the Spirit and Mary.* Wilmington, Del.: Michael Glazier, Inc., 1981.

Our Lady Speaks to Her Beloved Priests—The Marian Movement of Priests, Milan. St. Francis, Maine: National Headquarters, 1982.

Randall, John *et al. Mary: Pathway to Fruitfulness.* Locust Valley, N.Y.: Living Flame Press, 1978.

Rosage, David E. *Praying with Mary.* Locust Valley, N.Y.: Living Flame Press, 1980.

von Balthasar, Hans Urs. *The Threefold Garland: The World's Salvation in Mary's Prayer.* Translated by Erasmo Leiva-Merikakis. San Francisco: Ignatius Press, 1982.

NEW DIRECTIONS

Flanagan, Donal. *The Theology of Mary.* Butler, Wis.: Clergy Book Service, 1978.

Greeley, Andrew. *The Mary Myth: On the Femininity of God.* New York: Seabury, 1977.

Haughton, Rosemary. *Feminine Spirituality: Reflections on the Mysteries of the Rosary.* New York: Paulist Press, 1976.

Heft, James. "Marian Themes in the Writings of Hans Urs von Balthasar." *Marian Studies* 31 (1980), 40–65. Reprinted in part in *Communio* 7 (1980), 127–139.

Kenny, J.P. *The Meaning of Mary for Modern Man.* Melbourne, Australia, 1980.

Marian Seminar, 1980: Kenya (Nairobi), Zambia (Monze, Ndola). *Mary in Faith and Life in the New Age of the Church.* Dayton, Ohio: International Marian Research Institute, 1983.

Ruether, Rosemary. *Mary—The Feminine Face of the Church.* Philadelphia: Westminster Press, 1977.

Tambasco, Anthony J. *What Are They Saying About Mary?* New York: Paulist Press, 1984.

208th General Chapter of the Order of Servants of Mary. *Do Whatever He Tells You—Reflections and Proposals for Promoting Marian Devotion.* Edizioni Marianum Rome: General Curia OSM, 1983.

MARY IN DOCTRINE/HISTORY

Bouyer, Louis. *The Seat of Wisdom: An Essay on the Place of the Virgin Mary in Christian Theology.* New York: Pantheon Books, 1962.

Congar, Yves, O.P. *Christ, Our Lady, and the Church.* Westminster, Md.: The Newman Press, 1957.

de Lubac, Henri, S.J. *Splendor of the Church.* New York: Paulist Press, 1963. See chapter entitled "The Church and Our Lady."

Dictionary of Mary "Behold Your Mother." New York: Catholic Book Publishing Co., 1985.

Flanagan, Donal. *In Praise of Mary.* Dublin: Veritas Publications, 1975.

Gaffney, Patrick, S.M.M. *Mary's Spiritual Maternity According to St. Louis de Montfort.* Bay Shore, N.Y.: Montfort Publications, 1976.

Graef, Hilda. *Mary: A History of Doctrine and Devotion.* Two Volumes. London: Sheed and Ward, 1963.

Healy, Kilian, O. Carm. *The Assumption of Mary.* Wilmington, Del.: Michael Glazier, Inc., 1982.

Heft, James. "Papal Infallibility and the Marian Dogmas: An Introduction." *Marian Studies* 33 (1982), 47–89. Published also in *One in Christ* 18 (1982), 309–340.

Laurentin, Rene. *The Question of Mary.* Translated by I.G. Pidoux. New York: Holt, Rinehart, & Winston, 1963.

Meilach, Michael D., O.F.M. *Mary Immaculate in the Divine Plan.* Wilmington, Del.: Michael Glazier, 1981.

O'Carroll, Michael, C.S.Sp. *Theotokos: A Theological Encyclopedia of the Blessed Virgin Mary.* Wilmington, Del.: Michael Glazier, Inc., 1983.

Rahner, Hugo, S.J. *Our Lady and the Church.* New York: Pantheon Books, 1961.

Rahner, Karl, S.J. *Mary, Mother of the Lord: Theological Meditations.* New York: Herder & Herder, 1963.

Ratzinger, Joseph Cardinal. *Daughter Zion: Meditations on the*

Church's Marian Belief. Translated by John M. Mc-Dermott. San Francisco: Ignatius Press, 1983.

Schillebeeckx, Edward, O.P. *Mary, Mother of the Redemption.* Translated by N.D. Smith. New York: Sheed and Ward, 1964.

Suenens, Léon Joseph Cardinal. *Mary, the Mother of God.* New York: Hawthorn Books, 1959.

Vollert, Cyril, S.J. *A Theology of Mary* (Twentieth Century Encyclopedia of Catholicism). New York: Herder and Herder, 1965.

PASTORAL REFLECTIONS

Brown, R.E. "The Importance of How Doctrine Is Understood." *Origins* 10 No. 47 (May 7, 1981), 737–743. Keynote Address to the National Catholic Educational Association given on April 22, 1981.

Carberry, John Cardinal. *Mary, Queen and Mother: Marian Pastoral Reflections.* 1979.

Häring, Bernard, C.SS.R. *Mary and Your Everyday Life.* Liguori, Mo.: Liguori Publications, 1978.

Laurentin, René. *Our Lady and the Mass in the Service of the Peace of Christ.* Translated by Francis McHenry. New York: Macmillan, 1959.

National Conference of Catholic Bishops. *Behold Your Mother—Woman of Faith. A Pastoral Letter on the Blessed Virgin.* Washington, D.C.: United States Catholic Conference, 1973.

BIBLICAL PERSPECTIVES

Alfaro, Juan. "The Mariology of the Fourth Gospel: Mary and the Struggles for Liberation." *Biblical Theological Bulletin* 10 (January 1980), 3–16.

Bearsley, Patrick. "Mary the Perfect Disciple: A Paradigm for Mariology." *Theological Studies* 41 (1980), 461–504.

131

Blinzler, J. *Die Brüder und Schwestern Jesu* (SBS 21). Stuttgart: Katholisches Bibelwerk, 1967.

Bojorge, Horacio, S.J. *The Image of Mary According to the Evangelists.* Translated by Aloysius Owen, S.J. New York: Alba House, 1978.

Braun, Francois-Marie, O.P. *Mother of God's People.* Staten Island, N.Y.: Alba House, 1967.

Brown, R.E. *The Birth of the Messiah: A Commentary on the Infancy Narratives in Matthew and Luke.* New York: Doubleday & Co., Inc., 1977.

Brown, R.E., Fitzmyer, J.A., Murphy, R.E. *The Jerome Biblical Commentary.* Englewood Cliffs, N.J.: Prentice-Hall, Inc., 1968.

Brown, R.E., Donfried, K.P., Fitzmyer, J.A., Reumann, J., eds. *Mary in the New Testament: A Collaborative Assessment by Protestant and Roman Catholic Scholars.* Philadelphia: Fortress Press, 1978.

Brown, R.E. "Mary in the New Testament Writings." *America* (May 15, 1982), 374–379.

Brown, R.E. *The Virginal Conception and Bodily Resurrection of Jesus.* New York: Paulist Press, 1973.

Bultmann, Rudolph. *The Gospel of John.* Oxford: Blackwell, 1971.

Collins, Adela Yarbro. *Crisis and Catharsis—The Power of the Apocalypse.* Philadelphia: Westminster Press, 1984.

Deiss, Lucien. *Mary, Daughter of Sion.* Collegeville, Minn.: The Liturgical Press, 1972.

Feuillet, Andre. *Jesus and His Mother.* Still River, Mass.: St. Bede's Publications, 1984.

Fitzmyer, S.J., Joseph. *The Gospel According to Luke I–IX* (*Anchor Bible*, Vol. 28). New York: Doubleday & Co., 1981.

LaVerdiere, Eugene, S.S.S. *Luke—New Testament Message 5.* Wilmington, Del.: Michael Glazier, Inc., 1980.

McCoy, Marjorie Casebier. *Mary the Mother of Jesus.* (Bible Lives of Faith Series—Resource Book, Student Book). Nashville, Tenn.: Graded Press, United Methodist Publishing House, 1980.

McHugh, John. *The Mother of Jesus in the New Testament,* London: Darton, Longman and Todd, 1975.

Meier, John P. *Matthew—New Testament Message 3.* Wilmington, Del.: Michael Glazier, Inc., 1980.

Meyer, B. " 'But Mary Kept All These Things . . .' (Luke 2:19, 51)." *Catholic Biblical Quarterly* 26 (1964), 31–49.

Miguens, Manuel, O.F.M. *Mary "The Servant of the Lord": An Ecumenical Proposal.* Boston: St. Paul Editions, 1978.

Montague, George, S.M., "Behold Your Mother." *Marianist Resources Commission,* 12 Document 63 (February 1981), 3–10.

Thompson, William. "Matthew's Portrait of Jesus' Disciples." *Bible Today* (January 1981), 16–24.

MARIAN DEVOTION

Alonso, Joaquin María, C.M.F. *The Secret of Fatima: Fact and Legend.* Cambridge, Md.: The Ravengate Press, 1979.

Berselli, C. & Gharib, G., eds. *Sing the Joys of Mary.* Wilton, Conn.: Morehouse-Barlow Co., Inc., 1983.

Burnside, Eleanor Therese. *Bible Rosary: The Life of Jesus: Thirty-Five Mysteries.* Edited by Philip Gage, S.M. Birmingham, Mich.: Rosary Thirty-Five, 1981.

Carberry, John Cardinal. *The Book of the Rosary.* Huntington, Ind.: Our Sunday Visitor, 1983.

de Montfort, St. Louis. *The Secret of the Rosary.* Translated by Mary Barbour, T.O.P. Bay Shore, N.Y.: Montfort Publications, 1971.

Duff, Frank. *Miracles on Tap.* Edited by Denis McAuliffe. Bay Shore, N.Y.: Montfort Publications, 1961.

Hutchinson, Gloria. *Mary and Inner Healing. An Armchair Pilgrimage to Lourdes.* Cincinnati, Ohio: St. Anthony Messenger, 1980.

Laurentin, René. *Meaning of Lourdes.* Dublin: Clonmore & Reynolds, 1959.

Leies, Herbert F., S.M. *Mother for a New World: Our Lady of Guadalupe.* Westminster, Md.: The Newman Press, 1964.

Paul VI. *Apostolic Exhortation, Marialis Cultus: For the Right Ordering and Development of Devotion to the Blessed Virgin Mary.* Washington, D.C.: Publications Office, United States Catholic Conference, 1974.

Scriptural Meditations on the Rosary. Compiled by the Daughters of St. Paul. Boston: St. Paul Editions, 1981.

Scriptural Rosary: A Modern Version of the Way the Rosary Was Once Prayed Throughout Western Europe in the Late Middle Ages. Chicago: Scriptural Rosary Center, 1961.

Ward, J. Neville. *Five for Sorrow, Ten for Joy: A Consideration of the Rosary.* Garden City, N.Y.: Image Books, 1974.

ECUMENICAL PERSPECTIVES

Allchin, A.M. *The Joy of All Creation. An Anglican Meditation on the Place of Mary.* London: Darton, Longman and Todd, 1984.

Branick, Vincent P., ed. *Mary, the Spirit and the Church.* Ramsey, N.J.: Paulist Press, 1980.

de Satgé, John. *Down to Earth: The New Protestant Vision of the Virgin Mary.* Wilmington, N.C.: Consortium Books, 1976.

Farrell, Gerald J. and Kosicki, George W. *The Spirit and the Bride Say, "Come!"—Mary's Role in the New Pentecost.* Asbury Park, N.J.: AMI Press, 1981.

Perrin, Joseph-Marie, O.P. *Mary, Mother of Christ and of Christians.* Staten Island, N.Y.: Alba House, 1978.

Stacpoole, Alberic, ed. *Mary's Place in Christian Dialogue.* Wilton, Conn.: Morehouse-Barlow, 1982.

Thurian, Max. *Mary, Mother of All Christians.* New York: Herder & Herder, 1964.

MISCELLANEOUS

Cunningham, Lawrence. *Mother of God.* San Francisco: Harper & Row, 1982.

Domas, Mary Wirtz. *Mary U.S.A.* Huntington, Ind.: Our Sunday Visitor, 1978.

Appendix 1

Pondering Over in One's Heart the Sacred Word of God

Luke 2:19, 51

The following method of meditating on Scripture is an application of Mary's prayer.

Look into the points that are presented here in order to experience as Mary the Person of Jesus, the *Word*, who comes to us in a special way in the inspired text of the Bible, especially that of the Gospels and the Epistles of St. Paul. St. Jerome has strongly stated: "To be ignorant of the Scriptures is to be ignorant of Christ." The process of *Marian Reflection* may help all of us to become more aware of the presence of Jesus of Nazareth, the Son of God, and the Son of Mary, the Virgin of Nazareth.

"PONDERING OVER"

1. In biblical reflective prayer, we imitate Mary, the Mother of the Lord Jesus, who *pondered* over all these events in her heart.

2. Biblical prayer is a meditative reflection on the sacred word of God as it is written in the inspired text of the Sacred Scriptures, both the Hebrew Scriptures (the Torah, the Writings, the Prophets, the Psalms) and the New Testament. Cf. Psalms 1 and 39.

3. We open our eyes to the *texts* and allow the words to enter our minds and permeate our hearts.

4. We do this as believers united with a community of believers, as persons of faith who belong to a community of faith.

5. "The Word becomes Flesh" within us because of our faith and because of the Holy Spirit who is present.

6. These sacred words are also saving events for us because we know that God is ever present and faithful to his promises.

7. Through us the Word becomes flesh today in our times, in our world—our life has meaning because of the Word of life and we give meaning and life to the words by being and becoming through our faith living human instruments and witnesses of salvation.

8. We pause, we reflect on the biblical text and its meaning just as long as we feel so inclined; then we *calmly* move to the next phrase, word, thought, or image.

9. There is a message for me or for my family/community in this text to which I must constantly turn and then *reflect* again on it as an *event*—as a sacred experience in my life.

10. Throughout this meditative reading the *Presence of the Word* remains: "I am with you all through the days that are coming, until the consummation of the world" (Mt 28:20). He dwells among us as *Word Made Flesh:* "I am the Way, the Truth, and the Life" (Jn 14:16). "And Mary pondered in her heart the meaning of these events" (Lk 2:19, 51).

Appendix 2

References to Mary, Mother of Jesus

52-57 A.D. A. St. Paul reflects the background for Mary through his references to Jesus as being from the line of David, etc. Galatians 1:19; 4:4-5; 4:28-29; Romans 1:3-4; Philippians 2:6-7.

70 A.D. B. St. Mark has two passages dealing with Mary: Mark 3:31-35; 6:1-6a. Less probable passages: Mark 15:40, 47; and 16:1.

80-85 A.D. C. St. Matthew:
1:1-17—genealogy
1:18-25—Annunciation to Joseph
(Isaiah 7:14)
2:11, 13-14, 20-21
12:46-50
13:53-58

85 A.D.   D. St. Luke:
                        1:26-38—Annunciation to Mary
                        1:39-56—Visitation, Magnificat
                        2:1-21—Birth Narrative
                        2:22-40—Presentation in temple
                        2:41-52—Finding in temple
                        3:23
                        4:16-30
                        8:19-21
                        11:27-28—Blessedness of Mary

Acts of the Apostles: 1:14—Pentecost and last mention of Mary

90 A.D.   E. St. John:
                        1:13   —doubtful verse about Virgin Birth
                        2:1-12—wedding feast of Cana
                        6:42, 7:1-10; 7:41-43; 8:41—origins of Jesus questioned
                        19:25-28a—Calvary: Mary present standing at foot of cross

95 A.D.   F. Revelation (Apocalypse)—chapter 12 is highly *symbolic:* the woman is the Church rather than Mary, but possible relationship was intended by author.

HEBREW SCRIPTURES

All these references are more by accommodation than by strict interpretation. Texts are used more in liturgical celebration of Jesus and Mary. In all honesty they were not intended by authors to speak of Mary.

Genesis 3:15—Woman and the serpent
Isaiah 7:14
Isaiah 11:1
Zephaniah 3:14-17—Daughter of Zion

APOCRYPHAL GOSPELS

are much later 200-300 A.D. More imaginative and creative scenes from the life of Jesus and Mary. Mostly inaccurate.

Latin Pseudo-Matthew; Infancy Gospel of Thomas; Acts of Pilate or Gospel of Nicodemus; Gospel of Philip; Proto-Gospel of St. James; Apocryphal Acts of the Apostles; Gospel of Peter; Sibylline Oracles.